James D. S

OAKWOOD PRESS

CW01083767

SERVICE OF THE SOUTHERN RAILWAY

ITS CONSTITUENTS AND BR SOUTHERN REGION

by
R.W. Kidner
(including notes by David Gould)

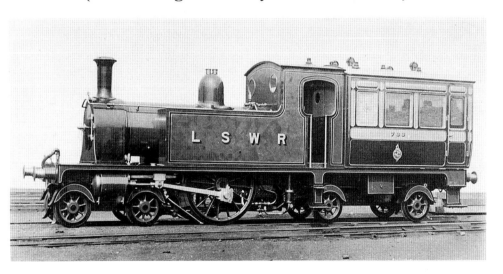

THE OAKWOOD PRESS

© Oakwood Press 1993

ISBN 0 85361 429 6

First published 1980
New enlarged edition 1993

Typeset by Gem Publishing Company, Brightwell, Wallingford, Oxfordshire.

Printed by Alpha Print (Oxon) Ltd, Witney, Oxfordshire.

*All rights reserved. No part of this book may be reproduced or transmitted
in any form or by any means, electronic or mechanical, including photo-
copying, recording or by any information storage and retrieval system,
without permission from the Publisher in writing.*

A train of LBSC double-cylinder lighting gas wagons running from Eardley Sidings
to Victoria, at Balham Intermediate about 1920; the locomotive is class 'I1' 4−4−2T
No. 3.   *R.C. Riley*

Title page: Drummond's well-known 'single' inspection car, built at Nine Elms in
1899, which became SR 58S in 1924.   *Lens of Sutton*

Published by
The OAKWOOD PRESS
P.O.Box 122, Headington, Oxford OX3 8LV

Contents

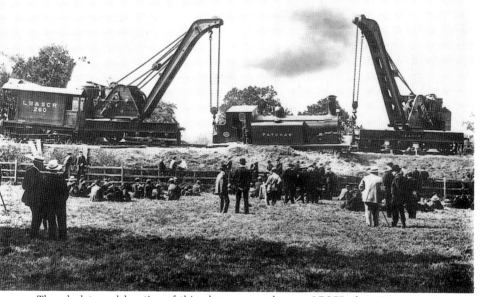

Though date and location of this photo are not known, LBSCR class 'D1' 0−4−2T No. 239 must have been well off the rails to need the ministrations of two heavy steam cranes.   *Lens of Sutton*

Introduction

The first notes for this book were made as long ago as 1928; at that time stock registers were not available, and much was conjectural. Only in recent years has there been much interest in Service Stock, and of course the most interesting vehicles have long since gone. It is hoped that this survey of them and their work will be found interesting to readers more conversant with the modern highly-technical service equipment. One thing is certain: number-taking was much easier when the principal inspection saloon was numbered 1S than today when it is TDB975025.

R.W. Kidner
1993

Acknowledgments

My first thanks must go to David Gould, who over the years has supplied items from the Vehicle Registers without which there would have been many errors and omissions. Thanks too to experts Gordon Weddell and Mike King whose knowledge is in many cases considerably superior to the author's and who have contributed generously. Also to Tom Burnham for extracts from SR Working Timetables, and to R.C. Riley for information and the loan of photographs, and to J. Smith of 'Lens of Sutton' whose photographs of 'forties stock have made this such a notable collection. Any errors or omissions in this rather complex book will be the fault of the author and not his contributors.

Strawberry Hill shed, LSWR, in 1923; the breakdown train at left comprises closed van No. 57S, match truck No. 63S, Crane No. 4 (Appleby 1875, later SR 33S), and 6-wheel brake van No. 56S.   *H.C. Casserley*

Chapter One
The Scene at Grouping

Railways have always needed vehicles of both passenger and goods type for their own internal purposes – that is to say, non-revenue-earning vehicles. In the early days they were few, as the engineering and traffic arrangements were not very complex. For example, early signalling needed little attention, and much engineering work was done on a local basis by contract. Of recent years the need has also been less, since road transport is used to carry workmen to the site of jobs, and with the network being reduced to mostly 'main' lines, the multiplicity of requirements for maintaining junctions, signal boxes, wharves, carriage depots and so on is much less. Thus it was only in the period from about 1880 to about 1945 that the very large fleets of service vehicles were needed.

The three railways which together with some minor ones made up the Southern Railway, the London & South Western, the London Brighton & South Coast, and the South Eastern & Chatham, all had similar kinds of service vehicles. The LSWR had an 'S' list, an 'LS' list for sludge tenders, another one for cranes; the LBSC had various lists, cyphered wagons, and some items with no observable number; the SECR had a large 'S' list and some other prefixes. The SR, instead of putting the tender lists together, for example, threw the whole lot into an 'S' and 'OS' list, in no particular sequence, except that to start with ex-LSW, SEC and LBSC vehicles were in that order. Other than that, a locomotive might be next in number to a wagon, a gas container to a crane. But it was very thorough; even an old frame if on wheels would have a number slapped on it.

Firstly and most importantly, there were the breakdown trains; the cranemakers had supplied all with the same kinds of heavy cranes, designed to fit within the load-gauge when travelling, and these were accompanied by one or two match-trucks, a riding van made from an old carriage, and a tool van adapted from a luggage van; these would remain permanently coupled at designated loco depots. Mess & Tool Vans were also to be found at all depots and on sites where major work was in progress; these were usually old third-brakes or guards vans. There were also stores vans, sometimes used statically, but more often lettered to run between named depots, to take sponge-cloths to a laundry, or to provide Signal & Telegraph depots with equipment from a main works. Station and bridge painting was a never-ending job, and vans for 'Outside Painters' were some of the most commonly-visible vehicles.

All three companies had large ports to serve; Newhaven and Southampton were railway-owned and used much specialised service stock, though wharf-side cranes (even on wheels) and many oil-storage tanks were left off the lists.

The Civil Engineers, of course, needed very many vehicles for track maintenance; some of these at Grouping appeared in various lists, but the Southern Railway created a separate list for them, prefaced by 'ED', which included ballast wagons, bolster wagons for rails, and ballast brakes and

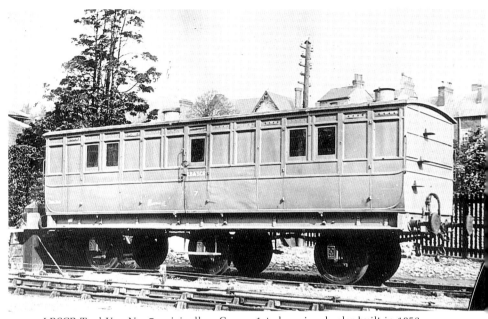

LBSCR Tool Van No. 7, originally a Craven 1st class six-wheeler built in 1853.

Lens of Sutton

A Stroudley 20 ft brake van attached to the Loco. Dept West Croydon.

riding vans, which were sometimes adapted carriages, but more often purpose-built.

Another type of vehicle given a place in the SR lists was the 'Yard Wagon'.
The most usual form was a stripped coach frame, and they were used at
locomotive and carriage works for moving materials and part-built items
around the premises.

A great many service vehicles are known only from a brief note in the
Registers, for there was a big clearance of old items in the three or four years
following Grouping, and in any case it was many years before railway
enthusiasts in general would take any note of such things. It would have
been nice to have seen No. 142S, for example, a six-wheeled SER post office
van built in 1859, but it went in 1925. What was probably the longest-
serving service vehicle was SR 173S, which started as one half of an SER
jointed eight-wheeler in 1851, was separated and became lamp-carriage No.
460 then SECR 0460 in 1905; it was withdrawn in 1929.

The Companies differed in their approach to departmental locomotives.
The LSWR originally formed a stud of them, but disbanded it and relied on
various small engines it happened to have acquired. The LBSC took tank
engines out of capital stock and lettered them for Locomotive Works usually
without a number, and took them back into capital stock later. The SECR
numbered its departmental engines in with the rest, even the two crane-
engines.

The LSWR was alone at Grouping in owning an engine-cum-saloon inspection car (though the LBSC had one earlier) but it does not seem to have
been in use at the time. The LSWR also had two Inspection/Directors'
saloons; the LBSC had a twelve-wheeler, as well as an eight-wheeled one
which the SR took on as a public saloon; the SECR Inspection Saloon, a
six-wheeler of 1886, SR 195S, was built as a public saloon and reverted to
this role soon after Grouping.

The LSWR and LBSC had electrified some suburban lines; the former had
taken over two small electric engines with the Waterloo & City Railway, and
one of these serviced the Company's power station at Durnsford Road. The
LBSC used overhead wiring, and fitted out two redundant petrol railcars for
work on it.

Of the minor companies, those in the Isle of Wight certainly had some
service stock, and a place for these was found in the 4XXS area of the SR list;
some vehicles were also taken over from the Somerset & Dorset Railway in
1930, though the Highbridge Works Train does not seem to have survived to
that time. The narrow-gauge Lynton & Barnstaple Railway did not acquire its
breakdown cranes until after Grouping.

Concerning the livery of service vehicles at the time of Grouping and after,
there seemed little uniformity. Mess & Tool (M&T) vans in SECR livery were
grey, LSWR ones were brown. Of two sludge tenders in LBSC livery at New
Cross, one was grey and one red. A relaying gang's M&T van at New Cross
was painted red as late as 1929. Of three ex-SECR vans noted in 1928, No.
0627S was red, 0635S was grey, and 0636S was brown, yet they were all
paintworks vans from Angerstein's Wharf. Of two sludge tenders at London

The Battersea Shed LBSC Tool Van was a Stroudley 3-compartment 3rd brake as built from 1872 to 1892.

Lens of Sutton

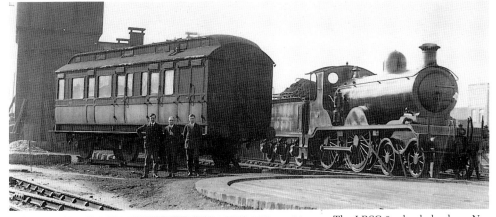

The LBSC 6-wheeled saloon No. 301 was used as the foreman's office at Bognor engine shed; seen here in February 1927.
H.C. Casserley

SECR Paintworks van No. S27, seen here as SR 0627S at Grove Park in April 1931; it was formerly a 2-compartment 3rd brake of 1862. *Author*

A South Eastern Railway 4-compartment 3rd, built by Gloucester C&W about 1865 became Paintworks van No. S65, modified with matchboard-sided lower panels, and roof rail for ladders etc.; here seen at Petts Wood in April 1932 as SR 0636S. *Author*

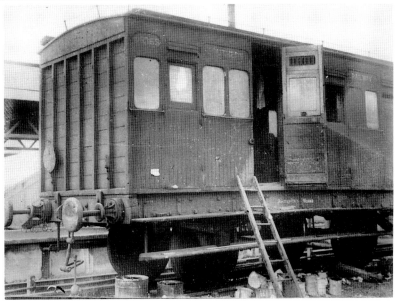

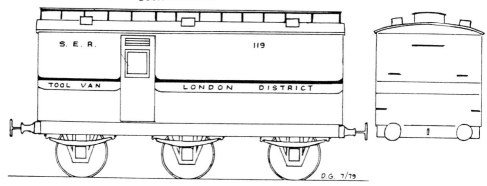

DOOR RECESSED.

S. E. R. 119

TOOL VAN LONDON DISTRICT

D.G. 7/79

This vehicle was photographed at Sevenoaks in 1884. It was formerly a P.O. van, built SER 1859. Official SR No.: 142S. Withdrawn 1925.
(Drawing not guaranteed for accuracy.)

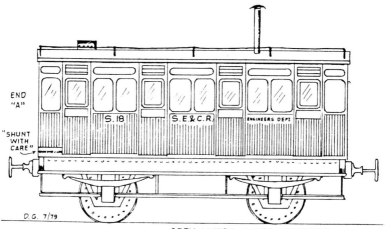

END "A"

"SHUNT WITH CARE"

S. 18 S.E.&C.R. ENGINEERS DEPT.

D.G. 7/79

GREY LIVERY, WHITE LETTERING.

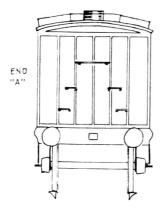

END "A"

Believed to be former SER 32-seat 'Enclosed Third', built by Gloucester RC&W Co. in 1864. Length over body: 19′ 6″. Width over body: 7′ 3″. Height, buffer centres to underside of cornice: 6′ 5¼″. Official SR No.: 0618S. Withdrawn June 1931.
(Drawing not guaranteed for extreme accuracy.)

David Gould

Bridge in 1929, No. 0989S was grey, but 501S was green. All the vans noted at Wimbledon Engineers Ironworks, were black in 1929, except No. 071S which was red. However, carriage lighting gas container wagons were always grey, and breakdown cranes were always red. The SECR also painted some of its mobile hand cranes red. Inspection saloons were green; as time went on some other service vehicles were also green because they were not re-painted on conversion; only the number was changed.

Track maintenance stock was painted 'red oxide', which was a kind of orange brown; this applied to ballast wagons, riding vans, bolsters, hopper wagons, and brakes.

It took about three years for the Southern to form a unified service stock list; it must have required much work 'on the ground'. There were a few cases where the new list could be lifted from old ones, such as the run of ex-SECR M&T vans, or ex-LBSC locomotive coal wagons, but mainly it seems to have been patiently built up. One can imagine that in 1925 the Western engineers asked for a small engine for Meldon Quarry, and ex-SECR 313 was renumbered 225S. Then it was decided to put the crane engines on the S list; in the interval some other items had been added, so they became 234/5S.

More than half the service vehicles were too old and decrepit for the SR to wish to keep them for long, so a duplicate OXXS list was made up, at that time much longer than the S list; 01S on was for ex-LSWR items, 0601S on for ex-SECR, 0901S on for LBSCR. The difference between the two lists is not obvious, for examples of every kind of vehicle apart from cranes could be found in both. The duplicate list did in general contain vehicles whose further life might be short; however not all guesses were correct, for No. 064S, an ex-LSWR 24 ft luggage van at Wimbledon ironworks, for example, was noted still around in the late 'forties.

Unfortunately railway enthusiasts showed no interest in service vehicles and almost no reports of sightings were published. In 1929 when the painters' van No. 0627S, a delightful little third brake of 1866, paid one of several visits to London Bridge Central side, observer G.T. Moody spotted it, but the *Railway Magazine* gave its number incorrectly as 06275 and reported the roof rails for carrying ladders as 'old time luggage railings' which would have made it very old indeed.

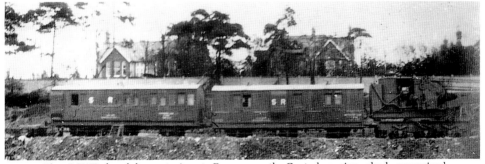

The LSWR breakdown train at Bournemouth Central engine shed comprised 6-wheeled 3rd brake No. 53S built 1891 (SR 036S), 6-wheeled guards van No. 55S (former 105 built 1888; SR 035S), and Heavy Crane No. 3 (Dunlop & Bell 1885, SR 32S) a six-wheeler with a lift of 38 tons; seen here outside the shed in 1932.

Author

LSWR No. 50S was a single-ended guard's van stationed at Barnstaple Junction shed as SR 035S, lettered 'Loco Department Barnstaple Junction, Western District. Load 2 tons, Tare 9.10.0.' Photographed 26th August, 1929. *Author*

This long-lived van, originally 1887 24 ft luggage van No. 5092, was from 1921 LSW 140S, a Machinery Van at Wimbledon depot. It is seen here at Queens Road in August 1949 as No. 064S. The notice on the side reads 'This vehicle is not to be shunted over hump sidings owing to valuable machinery'. *Author*

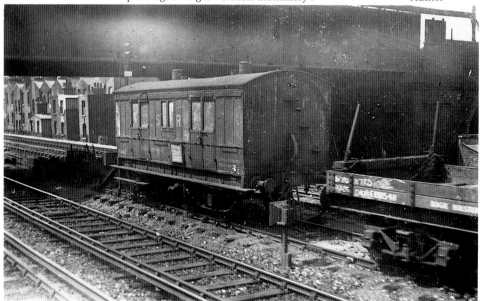

Chapter Two
Conversions of Passenger Stock

PASSENGER TRAIN VANS

In cases where the ordinary box-vans did not provide enough space for a service use, passenger luggage or guards vans were picked from the stock of superannuated vehicles more or less at random. Though there were some cases of one type being used in numbers at one time, more often it was varied; the following presents a summary of the types used, and more individual items will be found in the Appendices.

Ex-LSWR

Most LSWR breakdown trains included a 6-wheeled 30 ft van with centre guard's look-out in the roof, for example LSW 56S at Strawberry Hill, though the Bournemouth Central train used a similar type of van No. 53S but with side-duckets, built from 1888. Of the 22 ft 4-wheeled vans, a type with one-end duckets was noted in use in three cases, Nos. 035S, 079S and 081S; the luggage van version was typified by No. 064S. The only 18 ft luggage van became No. 919S. The 24 ft vans with semi-elliptical roof were considerably used, including the milk-van type; the 6-wheel version of this type was less used. Some 56 ft vans rebuilt in 1921 from ambulance vans also went to departmental use. Two Post Office vans were converted: the 1886 6-wheel No. 4904 to 566S, and 1898 bogie van 4911 to 1448S.

Ex-LBSCR

Although it is probable that some Craven 4-wheeled vans became service vehicles, no details are available. Of the Stroudley 4-wheeled vans with end duckets, 20 ft long over bodies, many became tool vans at locomotive depots; they were built between 1881 and 1891, and only one was in capital service by Grouping. Five of Stroudley's 26 ft 6-wheeled vans built during the same period were also converted, at least one being in departmental service in SR livery.

Of the Billinton 6-wheeled vans, 30 ft long and built from 1891 to 1906, very many were converted, remaining in use into BR days. This group of vans comprised guard's vans with centre duckets, parcels vans with no duckets, milk vans with slatted sides and ends, and guard's vans with duckets at each end. Only three of the last type were observed in departmental use.

Ex-SER and SECR

Of the little 18 ft passenger brakes, mostly with end 'birdcages' which ended their lives topping and tailing suburban sets, some 30 became service vans; they were built from 1851 to 1866. In the early 1870s a type with 26 ft body and centre 'birdcage' appeared, and some later became service vans. From 1888 32 ft vans, six-wheeled, were built, some with two pairs of end duckets, some with centre roof lookout, and both were still built well into SECR days, many ending up as service vans, including some 34 taken in

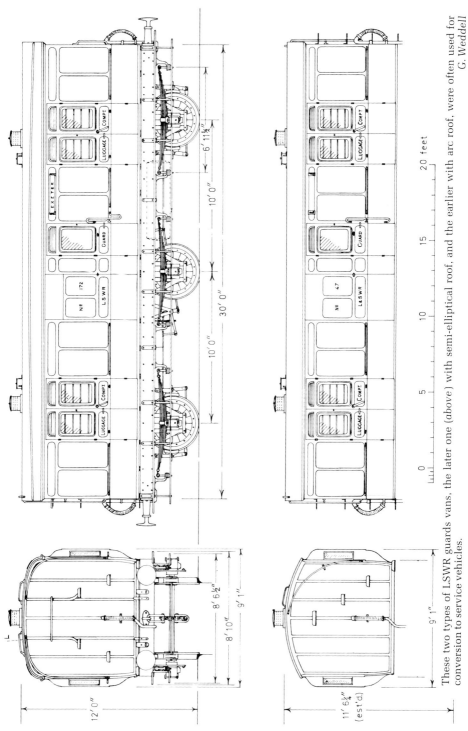

These two types of LSWR guards vans, the later one (above) with semi-elliptical roof, and the earlier with arc roof, were often used for conversion to service vehicles.

G. Weddell

The only 18 ft milk van the LSWR possessed, SR No. 1251, became 919S in 1935, lettered 'To work between Lancing and Brighton only'.

Lens of Sutton

A 30 ft 6-wheeled LSWR guard's van, built in 1896 and formerly SR No. 86, became 1348S in 1938, lettered 'Bridge Repairers, Wimbledon Ironworks', and also having the panel forbidding hump-shunting.

Lens of Sutton

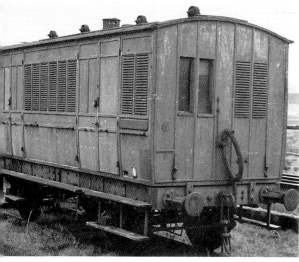

An ex-LCDR 'Guard Vitesse' perishables van, SECR 458, SR 1786, became No. 728S, for the Central Division Engineers Dept.

Lens of Sutton

1941 for ARP trains. Four postal vans were converted: SER No. 88 (4w.) to a tool van in 1902; No. 119 also, lasting to 1925; bogie van No. 4947 (1896) became an ARP Instruction Van, No. 1449S, in 1939; bogie van No. 4948 became a mess van 1537S in 1940. One SECR-built Maunsell PMV (No. 1977) became DS1026 in 1948.

Ex-LCDR

Of the early 4-wheeled vans with raised end look-outs, only three (one having lost its lookout) lasted as service vans into SR days, Nos. 0608 –0610S in Dover's breakdown train. The numerous 6-wheeled vans, 27 ft with centre roof observatory built from 1872 to 1886 (27 ft 2 in. up to 1878), and a similar type with side duckets were much used for service vehicles, and a later 28 ft type was massively plundered in the 1930s, some 23 examples being taken.

SR-built

Somewhat surprisingly, both Maunsell and Bulleid vans were beginning to be used before nationalisation. No. 1201 became rail-cleaning van 281S in 1939, though it reverted to capital stock later. No. 1072 became 748S in 1947; both were Maunsell luggage vans. Four Bulleid vans (4w.), Nos. 1787, 1791, 2127 and 2164 became 466/469/470/1S for use in week-killing trains in 1947.

CARRIAGES

Compartment stock could easily be transferred for use as riding vans, but most service uses required clear space, and often the compartment divisions were stripped out. Some, such as the SECR 3-compartment bogie 3rd brakes, did offer plenty of space. Usually all doors other than one or two were sealed, and lower footboards added to those left, unless already there. The greatest number of carriages used in SR days were of SECR origin, because few of these were taken for making up push-pull trains, as LBSC and LSWR ones were. Certain SECR types were not used, because they fitted into the scheme for reframing electric stock. The following gives a summary of the carriages converted to service use.

Ex-LSWR

The LSWR used old third brakes, both 4-wheeled and 6-wheeled, for inclusion in breakdown trains, but none of the high-roofed close-coupled stock, either 6-wheeled or bogie, was used. About 20 compos and third brakes were taken in late years, and some of the corridor stock built from 1905, mainly former restaurant cars, were used for ARP trains in 1942/3. In 1947–9 several 3rd and compo brakes of the ex-LSWR corridor stock were converted.

This SER 26 ft parcels van of 1875 became SR 1893, and was transferred to 473S in 1930, allocated to the Paintworks Dept., London East Division. Here it is in the siding by the London Bridge water tank.

Lens of Sutton

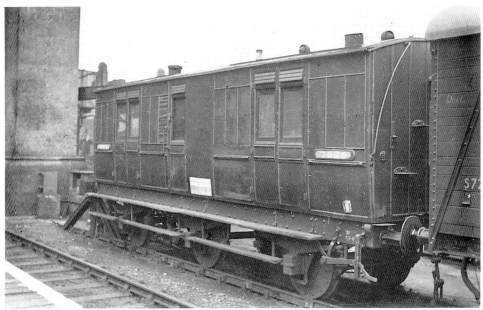

No. 762S was originally an LCDR 6-wheeled guard's van, No. 36 of 1887; it was SR 427 and from 1934 attached to Engineers Dept, London East Division, seen here at London Bridge. *Lens of Sutton*

A narrow six-wheeled guard's van built by the SER in 1897, which from 1939 was No. 1512S, an ARP Cleansing Van; here seen as an Engineers Dept M&T van incorrectly numbered DS1512S, about 1950. *Lens of Sutton*

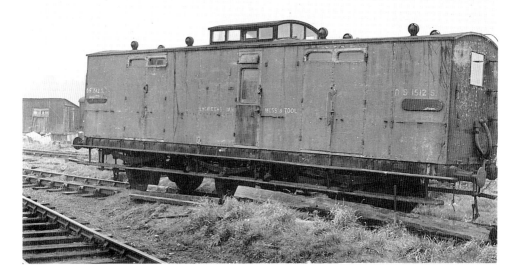

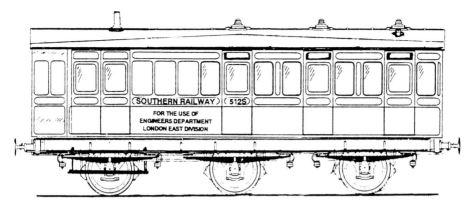

This Billinton 6-wheel 3rd brake of a type begun in 1893 lasted in Service use until 1933.

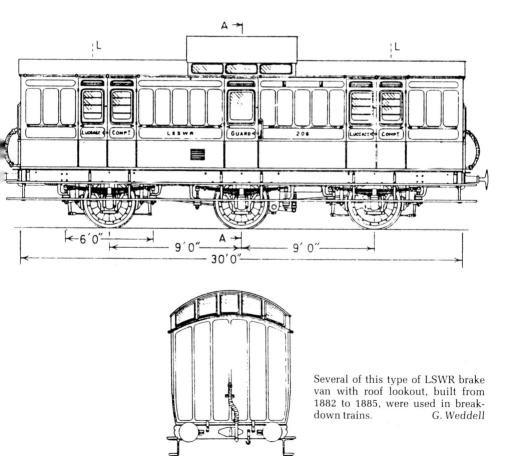

Several of this type of LSWR brake van with roof lookout, built from 1882 to 1885, were used in breakdown trains.   *G. Weddell*

A later type of SECR guard's van, built 1908, transferred in 1941 to 1619S for the Loco. Running Dept Feltham.
Lens of Sutton

Few of the 32 ft covered vans with end doors became service stock; this one, SR 4664 of 1905, was transferred in 1935 to 916S, Outdoor Machinery Dept, Three Bridges.   *Lens of Sutton*

Originally an SECR Postal Stowage Van No. 113, later SR Luggage Van No. 2021, this 1907 vehicle became 221S in 1945, lettered Engineers Dept Painting, London East Division. The number reads as DS225, but this is the result of painting DS221 on top of 221S.   *Lens of Sutton*

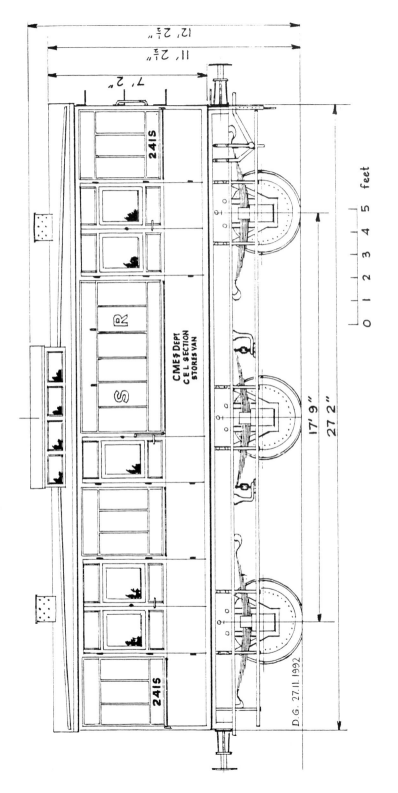

Ex-LCDR six-wheeled full brakes with centre roof lookouts were less common in Service use than similar ones with side duckets. This one had been LCDR No. 11, SECR 472, SR 394, becoming a stores van in 1929.

G. Weddell

This LBSC Stroudley guard's van of 1892, former SR 714, became 394S in 1929. *Lens of Sutton*

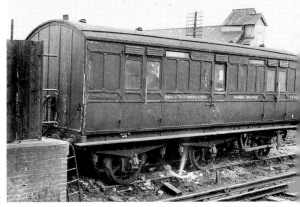

An LBSC Billinton parcels van, SR 2159, which in 1936 became 948S, seen here about 1950 as DS948, Signal & Telecommunications Dept stores van. *Lens of Sutton*

An LBSC Stroudley 3rd brake, seen here at East Croydon in May 1934 as Engineers Signals Dept Tool Van 01081S. *Author*

An arc-roofed SER 6-wheeled 2nd, SR 1459, built by Cravens in 1880, became 259S in 1929, 'for accommodation of relaying gang, Engineers Dept, Western Division'.

R.C. Riley

An early LCDR 3rd (No. 104) was transferred as 0816S to the Western Division and was noted at Barnstaple Junction in 1929; this later photo was taken at Exmouth Junction in 1946. *R.C. Riley*

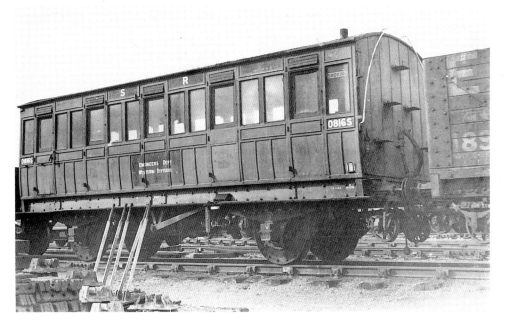

A riding van in the ED series, ED 62526 at Sevenoaks in February 1934; formerly LCD 3rd brake No. 122 of 1889; former SECR 1st, SR 7448 attached.   *Author*

Tool van 444S at Ryde IOW was formerly a North London Railway 3rd, and ran as IWR No. 44 until conversion; it is seen here in 1932 at St Johns Road shed.   *Author*

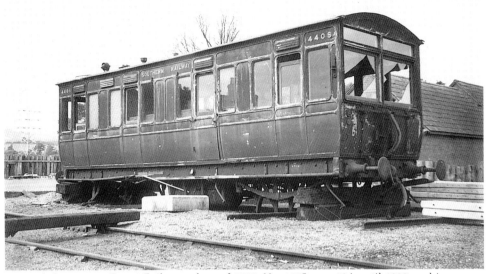

A Somerset & Dorset Railway saloon of 1885, No. 440S, was 32A until 1930, and is here seen at Broad Clyst after an accident in September 1947. *R.C. Riley*

A carriage with a varied history: built in 1881 by the LSWR as a bogie compo.; sold to the Plymouth Devonport & South-Western Railway (their No. 17); returned to the SR and sent to the IOW in 1923 as a third brake 4106; returned to the mainland and later transferred in 1941 to the S & T Department, Blackfriars, numbered 1630S. *Lens of Sutton*

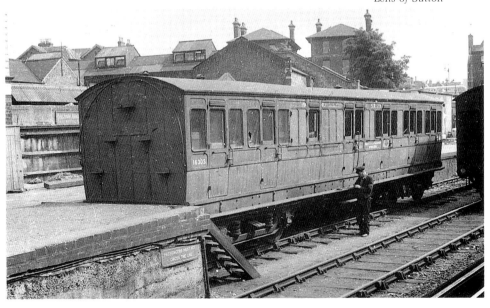

A once-exclusive SER 1st/2nd compo. built 1899, SR No. 867 when derated to 3rd class, was converted in 1943 to mess-room 1838S; fitted with corridor connectors when part of an ARP Cleansing Train, running between two ex-LSWR restaurant cars; the near end connector has been blanked off.

Lens of Sutton

An ex-SECR 50 ft saloon of 1905, SR 7920, once part of the Royal Train, as Temporary Office 1062S from 1948 at Wimbledon. *Lens of Sutton*

This ex-LBSC lavatory third body of 1900 was reframed in 1931, as SR 2177, and in 1940 became part of the Eastleigh breakdown train as 1543S. Note hand-rails painted white to help in the blackout. *Lens of Sutton*

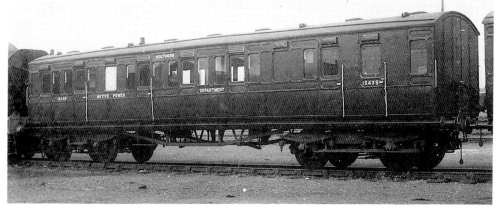

Ex-LBSCR

A number of Stroudley 4-wheeled 3rd brakes were used, and two were noted in SR days (01081S, and 0995S, the latter having match-boarded sides). Billinton 6-wheel 3rd brakes (30 ft) were used as M&T vans, and from the late thirties, a few bogie carriages. Of the 'balloon' type of Marsh stock, only four seem to have been used; these were at Lancing and were fitted with dumb buffers thus restricting them to depot use; these high-roofed coaches were outside the loading gauge on some lines.

Ex-SER and SECR

Of the very early stock, a few of the 1862 – 6 20 ft carriages, 4-compartment thirds and 2-compartment brakes, survived in Mess & Tool van and Outside Paintshops use in the SR days. A 3rd brake of 1866 had a very long life after conversion as SECR S27 and SR 0627S; when finally withdrawn in 1932, it became a grounded body at Bromley South. Of the 33 ft arc-roofed stock built from 1883 – 7 (6w.) two were noted as Engineers Dept vans on the Western Division (258/9S). Some 30 ft 1sts were used in cable-laying trains, and two 44 ft bogie compos went as service vehicles to Stewarts Lane (900/1S). A 33 ft 6-wheeled saloon as 0824S carried VIPs around the new Southampton Docks in the early 1930s. A bogie 2nd of 1900 went in 1939, and from then on all types of SECR bogie stock were taken, including four of the once-prestigous corridor birdcage compo brakes from the north-to-south inter-Company trains.

Ex-LCDR

The Managing Committee regarded LCDR stock as only fit to throw away, and the SR seem to have followed, using its 4- and 6-wheeled carriages for ballast brakes, M&T vans, or workmens trains. This included 30 ft stock rebuilt from 6-wheeled to 4-wheeled; three of these became workmens coaches 1050 – 2S in 1936. Most of the bogie coaches were sent to the IOW, but three were taken in 1933 for the Bricklayers Arms breakdown train, Nos. 725 – 7S.

Ex-SR

A large number of carriages are shown with service numbers in the Register because their frames were used as yard wagons or crane match-wagons. These are not dealt with there; however one frame must be mentioned, that of Maunsell coach No. 5537, burnt out before the War at Bourne-wood (Swanley), which was used in 1939 to build No. 1308S, a cinema van which with accumulator van No. 1309S (ex-LSWR 4w. luggage van) went around teaching the duties of the staff in the event of air-raids.

Some groups of 'carriage stock' service vehicles deserve attention:

WORKMENS' CARRIAGES

The stock for workmens' trains to industry, such as those to the East Kent coalfield, were not numbered in service stock, but those provided for the

Two of the former SECR corridor carriages for through services to the Midlands, SR 6625 (DS3193) and 6624 (DS3211) at Stewarts Lane as breakdown train riding vans in May 1959.   *R.C. Riley*

This ex-LSWR corridor saloon on 'ironclad' bogies formed part of the 1943 Clean Dressing trains, as 1834S. Here it is later, attached to a Maunsell luggage van as a mobile canteen, No. DS1026.   *Lens of Sutton*

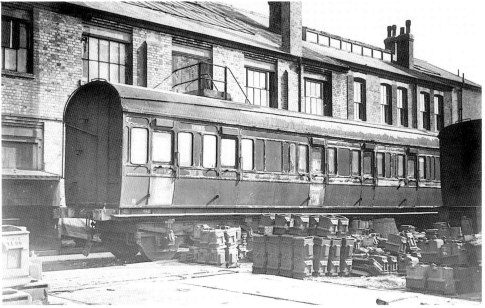

Few of the LBSC 'Balloon' type carriages were converted. This one, former 6275, now 1716S, and 6271 now 1635S were at Lancing Works, and both being fitted with dumb buffers, presumably never went outside. *R.C. Riley*

Stroudley 4-wheel 3rd No. 425 was first numbered 01138S in 1924, and in 1929 put in the Lancing Workmen's Train as 407S; note how the compartments were numbered throughout the train. *Lens of Sutton*

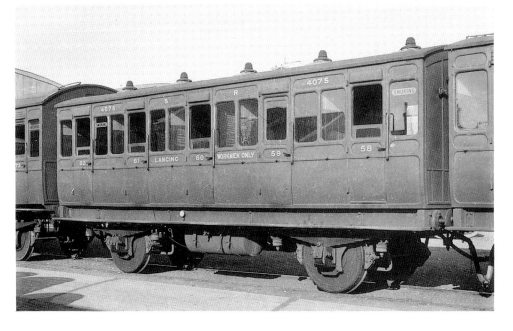

Later phases of the Lancing train: the second included this ex-LSWR 3rd brake No. 2646 as 413S (*above*), and the third one (*below*), DS70053, formerly SECR 10-compartment 3rd. No. 1067.   *Lens of Sutton*

Southern's own activities were. In 1934 three ex-LSWR bogie thirds were numbered 0853–5S to carry workers to parts of the new Southampton Docks, and another three (former 244/237/404) as 1298S 1300S in 1938 for the same purpose. Three ex-LCD 4-wheeled (former 6w.) coaches which became 1051–3S in 1936, and were unofficially lettered 'Pirelli Staff Only' were used at Fratton. There was a workmen's coach in the IOW, which may have gone down from Ryde to the Medina Wharf with the early coal empties.

The best-known train however was that provided for workers at the Lancing carriage building and repair depot, of which there were three generations of stock. Up to 1934 it was made up from 4-wheeled carriages, painted brown, with each compartment numbered down the train; short buffers were fitted except at the ends. The stock available was: 395S–401S (Billinton 1904), 402S–409S (Stroudley, former 01133–40S) and 410–6S (Billinton 1904). An ex-LCD 4-wheel 3rd brake of 1888 (3067), originally renumbered 01162S, was renumbered 417S in 1930 and added to the train.

From 1934 twelve various ex-LSWR bogie carriages were used:

401S cpo bk 6418	405S 3rd 331	409S 3rd 211
402S 3rd 351	406S 3rd 420	410S 3rd 435
403S cpo 4752	407S 3rd 425	411S 3rd 368
404S cpo 4786	408S 3rd 269	413S 3rd bk 2646

A later train (1960) comprised:

DS 70052	SR (SECR 10 Compt 2nd) 1067
DS 70053	SR (SECR 10 Compt 2nd) 1089
DS 70054	SR (SECR 10 Compt 2nd) 970
DS 70061	SR 'Ironclad' 2nd brake 3208
DS 70062	SR rebodied LSW 9-compt lav. 2nd 253
DS 70063	SR rebodied LSW 9-compt lav. 2nd (compts 39–47) 329
DS 70064	SR (SECR 10 compt 2nd) 1087
DS 70065	SR (SECR 10 compt 2nd) 1063
DS 70066	SR (SECR 10 compt 2nd) 1105
DS 70067	SR (SECR 10 compt 2nd) 1112
DS 70068	SR 'Ironclad' 2nd brake 3207
DS 70080	SECR 2nd brake no roof lookout 3473 (spare)

DS70200, an experimental all-plastic carriage built in 1963 as a prototype non-corridor suburban coach, was also on the train for a time (compartments 39–48) but later ran as S1000S, and ended up on the private East Somerset Railway. The train was stored overnight at Hove; the early stock was lettered 'Lancing Workmen Only' and the 1960 one 'C&W Workmens Coach, Lancing Works'.

WAR TIME ARP VANS

On 29th June, 1939 the SR exhibited at Waterloo a pair of vans painted bright yellow with the slogan 'We've Got to be Prepared'. They were two postal vans, an ex-LSWR one of 1898 (1448S), and ex-SECR 4947 (1449S) of 1896.

The air-raid precautions programme called for a number of 6-wheeled guard's vans to be used as cleansing vans; in November 1939 twenty-three (1506–22S, 1527–30S and 1535/6S) were converted to either cleansing or mess vans (see Appendix) and in 1941 more were used (1601–14S); the first of these was later sold to the Derwent Valley Railway and finally moved to the Bluebell.

SR stock was also used for three 'Casualty Evacuation Trains' but these were not given departmental numbers. ARP Breakdown Vans 1438–40S were ex-SECR 6-wheeled vans which became Government property, though returned to the SR in August 1943. Six others (1441–6S) were converted from ex-LSWR elliptical-roof luggage vans. In 1943 eight of the postal vans, which were not now being used, were turned over to ARP storage (see Appendix).

Also in 1943 some ex-SECR 6-wheeled vans were paired with former LSWR dining cars as 'Clean Dressing Vans' (see Appendix).

In 1945 a need arose for temporary office accommodation at Wimbledon station; No. 1450S, former covered carriage truck (6w.) which had been converted in 1939 to an M&T van, was sent there together with a former LSWR dining car, by now a 'nondescript' saloon.

CABLE LAYING TRAINS

When the SR electrification programme was at its height in the 1930s, there was a fair amount of service stock devoted to this only.

In October 1931 a former SER 6-wheel 3rd, SR No. 1550, was renumbered 598S and used for staff conveyance in connection with cable-laying for London–Brighton electrification in the London area; in April 1932 No. 1579 was diverted to the same purpose, becoming 612S. (See also cable-laying wagons, Chapter 3.)

A cable train noted at Sevenoaks in March 1934 contained an ex-LCD 4-wheel 3 compt 3rd Bk. No. ED62526; this was one of four old carriages used for conveying plate-laying staff which was numbered in the ED stock and not the S stock on conversion in 1927. In addition there was an ex-SER 6-wheel 5 compt 1st still in green livery. In that year some service stock for cable-laying was created, as follows:

> 771S, formerly SECR van No. (SR) 551, allotted to 'Sevenoaks Cable Train'
> 772S, formerly SECR 6w. 1st No. (SR) 7417 allotted to 'Sevenoaks Cable Train'
> 773S, formerly SECR 6w. 1st No. 7448 allotted to 'Sevenoaks Cable Train'
> 777S, formerly SECR van No. (SR) 576 allotted to 'Eastbourne Cable Train'
> 778S, formerly SECR van No. (SR) 553 allotted to 'Eastbourne Cable Train'
> 779S, formerly SECR 6w. 1st No. 7474 allotted to 'Eastbourne Cable Train'
> 780S, formerly SECR 6w. 1st No. (SR) 7413 allotted to 'Eastbourne Cable Train'

Apart from these specific uses, most passenger stock was used either for stores transference, M&T (mess and tool) vans for the Locomotive Dept., Engineering Dept (sometimes C&W Dept was added), Outside Paintworks, Engineer's Ironworks, CEL (Carriage Electric Lighting) charging vans, or

The Sevenoaks cable train at work on 4th March, 1934 (see text). 'H' class 0–4–4T No. 1553 with ED62526 and 773S, still painted as First No. 7448.   L.T. Catchpole

The Bricklayers Arms breakdown train passing New Cross on 29th June, 1935: ex-LCD bogie stock, *left to right*, 726S (SR 859), 727S (862), 725S (854), all 42 ft composites altered to 3rd. Later at Hither Green, No. 727S finally had its body grounded at Bournemouth.

One coach of the Highbridge Works breakdown train, ex-LSWR corridor brake 321, converted in 1940 to 1573S.
Lens of Sutton

This SR Cinema Coach was built in 1939 on the chassis of a burnt out composite, No. 5537: 1308S, seen here with generator van 1309S, ex-LSWR 4w. LV, now on the Bluebell Railway.
Lens of Sutton

'Signal & Telecommunications'. Although some carried nothing but their number, most were fairly informative. Examples are: 392S (ex-LBSC 6w. GV) lettered 'Central Division No. 2 Extra Gang'; 512S, an ex-LBSC 3rd Bk., lettered 'For use of Engineers Department London East Division' with 'Mess & Tool Van' on the sole-bar. Ex-LCDR 4-wheel 3rd ED62525 had 'Eastern Division, Ashford, Kent, No. 1 Ballast Train' on its side, with the number on the sole bar.

No. 1345S (an ex-LSWR 6w. GV) was one of several carrying a notice requesting that it be not 'shunted over hump sidings'; this was never painted on, but appeared on a square or oval board screwed to the side; however, No. DS136, an ex-SECR 7-compartment lavatory 3rd brake, did have 'Not to be loose-shunted' in large letters on the brake end.

One sometimes came across former passenger vehicles with no identification at all, such as an ex-LSWR milk van which stayed for many years at the far end of the Newhaven West Quay siding; in sidings on the south coast were several decayed ex-SECR 4-wheeled GVs carrying simply a name, Portsmouth, or Brighton, probably left over from war-time use.

There was no uniformity in the positioning or style of lettering; some had two numbers as hasty overpainting faded.

An ex-SECR lavatory brake of 1910, SR 3363, was used to make this rather elaborate tunnel-clearance testing template vehicle in 1954; it was numbered DS22, and was later sold to the KESR. *Lens of Sutton*

These tiny but solid former SER 15 ft 5 in. box-vans were much used for service work. This one, lettered 'London (East) Division Engineers Electrification Dept.' has not had its S number (222S) painted on; note four 'torpedo' roof ventilators and wooden buffer faces. Photographed at London Bridge on 11th November, 1932. *Author*

Vacuum cleaner van No. V3 at Maze Hill in 1929; formerly LSWR 24S, it has two oil lighting pots, and was entered through a door at the left hand end using steps fixed over the buffers; there was also a sliding panel on each side. *R.H.C. Brousson*

Chapter Three
Departmental Wagons

Such covered trucks as were transferred to the departments were mainly used as stores vans. The Southern had 24 depots:

Angerstein's	East Croydon	Guildford	Southampton
Bricklayers Arms (2)	Eastleigh	Lancing	Salisbury
Ashford	Exeter	Longhedge	Twickenham
Brighton	Faversham	Newhaven	Waterloo
Chatham	Folkestone	Newport IOW	Wimbledon
Dover	Fratton	Portsmouth	

All specialised: the three Loco Works and Lancing in CME spares, Angerstein's, East Croydon and Wimbledon in Civil Engineers' materials, Southampton and Newhaven in docks equipment, and so on. While much of the stores distribution was via the guard's van of passenger trains, where the traffic was heavy special vans were allocated, sometimes painted with the points between which it was supposed to work, or confining it to a certain area such as Southampton Docks or Lancing Works. Others were just painted for the District they worked in.

All types of closed wagon were used; the most fascinating were the little square SER box-vans with roof ventilators and Mansell wheels. Because of their sound construction, some went on in use to the late 1930s.

Some open wagons transferred to service use were not distinguishable from 'traffic' except by having an 'S' number; for example the 80 or more 8 ton opens used by the LBSC for loco coal and ashes. The Eastern Division had an inordinate number of 'yard wagons' at Ashford and Angerstein's, but these were almost all stripped carriages, which were also used for carriage lighting gas containers (see separate section).

Some vans and trucks worked between Lancing and Mitcham Junction, where the Engineering Department had a yard for stripping old coach chassis and other vehicles; the wheels were sent to Lancing or Eastleigh for re-tyring. There was also a large space on which complex track layouts were made up, laid down, and then taken up again for transport to a site; a similar area existed at the New Cross Gate PW depot.

A number of service wagons were placed in a 61XXX number series; the latter part of this was used for ballast stock, but the lower numbers included various items, such as Nos. 61381–3, water tanks in the IOW. It also included shunting trucks (see later). A somewhat outlandish 'vehicle' was No. 61059, a well-wagon with a large transformer permanently built in, located at Brighton.

The wagon stock in the 'OS' and 'S' lists defies categorisation in most cases; its origins and purposes were so diverse. For example Nos. 0735 –0742S includes eight differing vehicles (one being an ex-LCDR 1882-built covered van, SECR 10277) and for differing jobs, 0724S (ex-SECR S31) was a tunnel examination wagon. The SECR had a series of works vehicles prefaced by a 'W'; this mainly comprised yard wagons made from coach frames, but not all; Nos. W85–7 were old SER 15 ft coal wagons, which must have

This ancient LBSC van, lettered 'Lancing Works Only' was fitted with a wooden brake block on one axle only. *Lens of Sutton*

Covered goods wagon No. 45465, SECR 1912, became 1904S in 1944 for the Loco. Dept at Exmouth Junction. *Lens of Sutton*

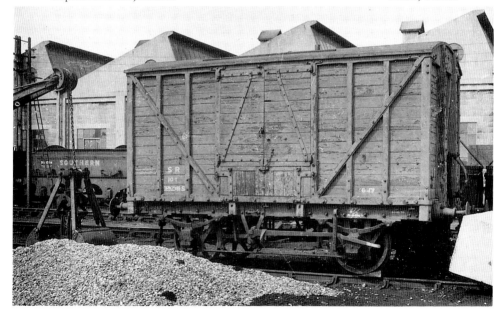

been 'lost' for a time, as the Register in giving them 0761–3S numbers, notes 'not previously included'. There was also a duplicate list of SECR wagons, which the SR swept into the OS list; for instance Nos. 02375 and 04502 were 1864/5 Brown Marshall open wagons, 0766S and 0767S. To make matters more confusing still, on either side of these in the Register lay 0765S, described as 'Yard Wagon W89', and 0768S, which was a 6-wheeled coach frame described as 'Yard Wagon 89'. The SR obviously did a good job in getting all these oddities on record, but it is hard to see a plan; they must just have been added as they cropped up.

There were however some categories of van conversions which were kept separate, and one such was Vacuum Cleaner Vans.

VACUUM CLEANER VANS

These vans contained petrol-driven air-pumps for providing vacuum cleaning of carriage upholstery in carriage sheds. The LSWR had numbered theirs 23–27S, and these first became SR 024–27S. The SECR also had some numbered S42–5 and S70, SR 0746–50S. However in 1929 they were removed from the lists, several being scrapped, and the remainder placed in a separate V list. They were made up from various covered wagons, with windows at ends and sides; no two of those actually seen were alike.

V1   From ex-LSW Covered Goods SR No. 43575; equipment taken from vacuum cleaner van SR 0750S, 1928. Stationed at Eardley. Withdrawn April 1934.

V2   From LBSC guard's van No. 369. Stationed at New Cross Gate. Withdrawn Sept. 1930; equipment transferred to ex-LSW covered goods No. SR 43409, which became new V2; withdrawn March 1934.

V3   From ex-LSW vacuum cleaner No. 24S; equipment taken from SEC vacuum cleaner S42, 1927. Stationed at Maze Hill, later Grove Park. Withdrawn May 1938.

V4   From ex-LSW vacuum cleaner 23S (SR 024S), Dec. 1929. Stationed at Ramsgate, later Eardley. Withdrawn Dec. 1937.

V5   From LSW covered goods No. 14439 and equipment from vacuum cleaner SR 0785S, March 1928. Stationed at Brighton, later New Cross Gate. Withdrawal date unknown.

V6   From LSW covered goods No. 14434 and equipment from LBSC vacuum cleaner No. 366, 1928. Stationed at Victoria. Withdrawn May 1938.

V7   From SR 0749S, which was ex-LSW covered carriage truck No. 057 with equipment from SEC vacuum cleaner van S45; renumbered V7 June 1930. Stationed at Bournemouth West. Withdrawn June 1936.

V8   From LSW vacuum cleaner 26S, Oct. 1929. Stationed at Eastleigh. Withdrawn Feb. 1932; equipment transferred to ex-LSW covered carriage truck SR No. 4507 which became new V8. Withdrawn March 1940.

V9   From LSW vacuum cleaner No. 27S, April 1930. Stationed at Exeter. Withdrawn April 1934.

Each van had two cleaning attachments. Nos. V1/2/4/6 each had a reciprocating twin cylinder pump with ring valves; V3/5/7/9 each had a reciprocating single cylinder pump with Poppet valves; V8 had a single cylinder pump with ring valves. There were also two electric vacuum cleaner vans V21 and V22.

A former IWR guard's van, which as 445S (based at Ryde St Johns Rd) served as a travelling tool van.   *Lens of Sutton*

A standard SR covered goods wagon adapted to a Pooley's Weighing Machine service van, DS483.   *Lens of Sutton*

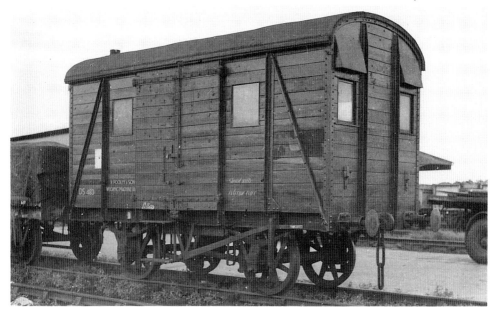

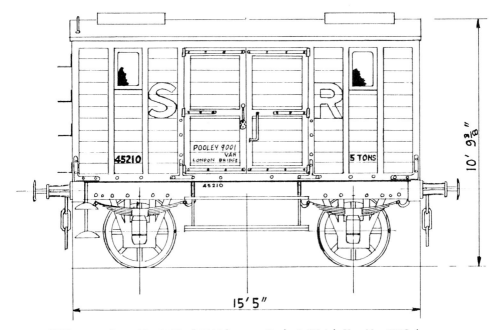

0 1 2 3 4 5 feet

SECR covered van No. 9169 of 1899 became Pooley's Weigh Van No. 223S; here as it appeared in 1932 it still carries its SR number 45210; note two sets of steps.

Van V6 was made up from LSWR covered van 14434, and is here shown as it was at Victoria carriage sidings until 1938.   *(Both) David Gould*

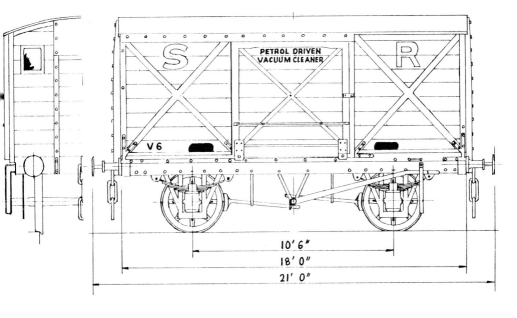

POOLEY'S WEIGH-VANS

These vans contained tools for servicing weighing equipment on hire from Messrs H. Pooley & Son Ltd of London. Three were noted: 223S, former SR box-van No. 45210; this was of the standard SER type with external vertical framing and centre doors; glazed roof-lights were added. The others were Nos. 482/3 high-roofed box vans with two windows in each side and one window at each end: lettered 'Pooley & Sons Weighing Machine Van'. These two vans were post-war conversions. Later Pooley's weigh-vans in service with BR were Nos. DS 70025 and DS 70263–5, converted from utility vans.

TELEPHONE EXCHANGE VANS

Nos. 1759S and 1762S were converted for this purpose from 6-wheeled horse boxes Nos. 3316 and 3317 (built LBSC 1907) in Sept. 1942 and withdrawn in 1945. They would have been for maintaining railway communication in the event of telephone centres being bombed out. It is believed they were lettered 'Engineers Section, S & T Section. Not to be worked in goods trains'.

CABLE-LAYING WAGONS

In the mid-thirties a number of 12-ton high-side wagons were adapted for cable-laying trains, by having drum-holders fitted, with ports at the ends for feeding cable through. After some 60 had been put in service, it was found preferable to have the ports at the ends of the sides; they kept their numbers, which were in a range from 29079 to 36897, and by 1942 all reverted to normal use. After the War 60 more were converted, with side ports, and given S or later DS numbers, including DS1657–83, DS1689–1713; later some more were converted but kept their numbers with a DS prefix.

SHUNTING TRUCKS

These wagons, called 'runners' on some other railways, were flat wagons with running boards and stanchions all round, which were interposed between locomotive and first carriage when shunting large sidings; they gave the driver a better view, and provided something safe for the man with the coupling-pole to hang on to. Those taken over at Grouping were first given S numbers, but soon moved to the 61XXX series, as follows:

61321	former 075S, ex-LSWR
61322/3	at Clapham Carriage Sidings
61324/5	bogie shunting trucks for Dover ferry, withdrawn c.1942
61326/7	at Bournemouth West
61328/9	bogie trucks for Dover Ferry, replacing 61324/5
61341–8	at various ex-SECR locations, former 180–191S
61361	ex-LBSC wagon allocated to Brighton lower yard

This former SECR ballast wagon No. 4298 was fitted with brushes between the wheels for clearing snow etc. and as 226S served at Feltham yard lettered 'Signal & Telegraph Dept Brush Truck Feltham'; photographed on 12th May, 1934.   *Author*

This 8-ton coal wagon built by the LBSC in 1905 (No. 6902) was one of about 100 which supplied locomotive coal to various Central Section engine sheds.
Lens of Sutton

MATCH TRUCKS FOR 'TUBE' STOCK

The LSWR required match trucks to couple up to Waterloo & City stock needing to go to Eastleigh for repair; the SR also required them for the later stock, some cars of which went to Selhurst for servicing. More such wagons were needed after it was decided to use surplus LTE 'tube' stock in the Isle of Wight, for moving it to mainland service depots and for route-testing and delivery. One of these vehicles noted was a conversion of 10-ton wagon S22796; the buffers at one end were sawn off at the stock, and a dropped buffing plate and coupler fitted between two heavy wooden uprights strongly bolted to the buffer beam. Control jumpers were fitted.

When the first 'tube' carriage arrived at Ryde St. Johns Road (on a road low-loader) it was immediately coupled to a mate, former covered van now DS 46951, newly lettered 'Match Wagon, Testing LT Stock'. Its first tests were behind a steam engine (4th September, 1966) but later diesel engine No. D2554 took over, after its arrival in October 1966. At the same time, a number of former Eastern Region 4-wheeled flats were equipped with continuous braking in Ryde Works to provide a train for lifting useable rails and points from closed sections.

A 'tunnel blocking wagon' for use in case of invasion, at Folkestone Junction on 10th June, 1946. It is fitted with an extra axle to take the weight of the concrete block inside, and all springs are wedged.   *N. Wakeman*

Chapter Four
Gas Wagons and Old Tenders

The use of travelling gas containers for carriage lighting was necessitated by the fact that while a great many carriages could be rostered to work into main carriage depots where gas was produced, stored and piped to the various sidings, there were some, especially those used on branch workings, which could not do so. The travelling containers were large cylinders (originally of rivetted construction, but later welded) mounted on old carriage frames. Mr Surrey Warner of the LSWR, contributing to *Railway Mechanical Engineering* in 1923, stated that the 'travelling gas storeholders' comprised either one vessel 20 ft long by 6½ ft diameter, or two measuring 18½ ft by 4 ft 2 in. mounted side by side; they carried from 4000 to 6500 cu. ft of gas at 11 atmospheres pressure.

Most companies made their own oil-gas; however the Isle of Wight Central Railway used compressed town gas.

The gas vessels were (in SR days) painted grey with large white numerals in the S or OS series, and in smaller letters the places to which it should be consigned when empty or full were given, the latter being its 'station' and the former the nearest gas producing depot. They were sometimes worked at the tail of a passenger train (all were piped) but more often in parcels or empties trains, and in complete trains of containers. The vessels were mounted on various 4-wheeled and 6-wheeled coach frames (and at the end of the SR era a few on short bogie frames); running boards were retained, and a lower running board at the valve end; handbrakes were fitted.

The depots to which empty containers were to be sent included Eastleigh, Clapham Junction, Rotherhithe Road (Bermondsey), and Brighton; points to which full containers were worked included Exeter Queen Street, Salisbury, Dover Marine, Charing Cross, Maze Hill, and Lancing. Towards the end of the SR era only the destination for empty containers was indicated.

The container wagons began to be built as soon as oil-lighting was generally discarded, in the late 1880s. The LSWR had a large number. The LBSC purchased some from the Metropolitan and Metropolitan District Railways when these turned over to electric lighting; the LBSCR had fewer gas-lit coaches and therefore fewer container wagons. It is difficult to give a concise run-down on these vehicles, though they are covered in the registers, because of frequent exchanges of cylinders and replacement of frames when these were condemned. Although the earlier cylinders were of rivetted construction and the later ones welded, this gave no indication of the age of the frame, and some rivetted cylinders were still being reframed in BR days. In the early years of the Southern Railway, at a time when the author took notes which can confirm or amplify the register, the following was the general position:

01S–019S:	ex-LSW 4w. (approx. 24 ft) with single cylinders all on Western Section
020S–023S:	ex-LSW 6w. double cylinders
66S–73S:	ex-LSW 6w. single cylinders

Former LSWR gas-container wagon No. 015S at Clapham Junction on 11th April, 1931, lettered 'Full to Salisbury, Empty to Clapham Junction'. This is a single welded-type cylinder mounted on the frame of a 4-wheeled postal van No. 4901. *Author*

A pair of rivetted-type cylinders mounted on a six-wheeled carriage chassis; originally LSWR of 1887, then SR 88S on the underframe of fruit van OE55, it was renumbered 2078S in 1946. *Lens of Sutton*

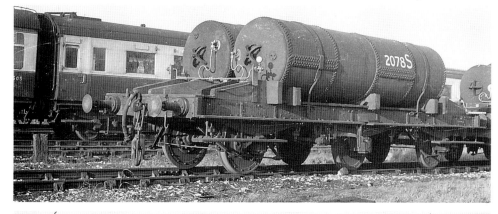

A train of empty gas-container wagons from Dover to Rotherhithe Road at St Mary Cray Junction in 1937; hauled by '01' class 0−6−0 No. 1388. *Author*

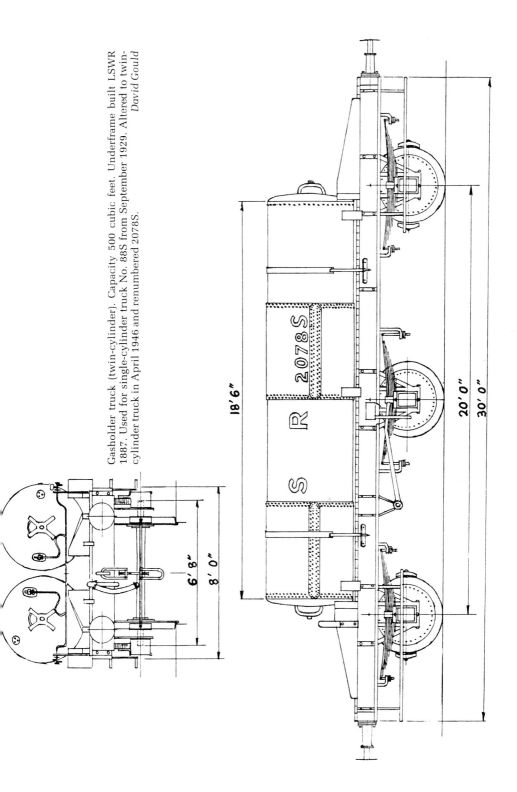

Gasholder truck (twin-cylinder). Capacity 500 cubic feet. Underframe built LSWR 1887. Used for single-cylinder truck No. 88S from September 1929. Altered to twin-cylinder truck in April 1946 and renumbered 2078S.

David Gould

18'6"

20'0"

30'0"

6'8"

8'0"

S R 2078S

Gas-container wagon No. 2014S comprised a tank from Eardley Gasworks mounted on a 33 ft underframe of an LSW saloon in 1933; formerly No. 292S.   *Lens of Sutton*

Gas-container 2052S photographed in 1949 has two rivetted tanks re-mounted on a short bogie frame.   *Lens of Sutton*

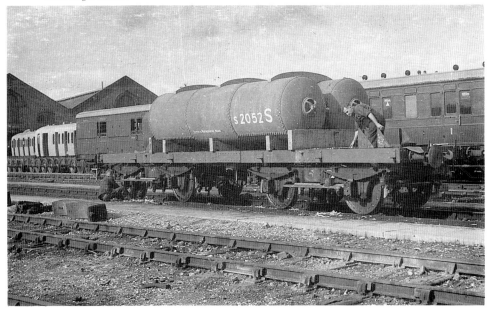

88S–90S:	ex-LSW 6w. single cylinders
121S–137S:	ex-SECR 6w. (28 ft) double cylinders, in process of being reframed on ex-LSW 6w. frames, mostly as singles
292S–297S:	ex-LBSC 4w. (24 ft) double cylinders, in process of being reframed on LSW 30–33 ft frames
01065S–01073S:	6w. double, apparently the remaining ones from the Met. and MDR purchase, in use on Central and Eastern Sections

The SECR had a number series, the lowest noted being No. 95 and the highest 217. Many of these cylinders later ran on LSWR frames; for example SECR No. 97 had its frame condemned in 1927 and one cylinder went on to the frames of LSWR 3rd. No. 2 as 66S and the other the frame of LSWR 3rd No. 056, to become 123S.

In 1936 two new vehicles were made up, Nos. 1048S and 1049S (later 2004/5S) using the frames of LSWR GVs Nos. 33 and 32.

The impossibility of presenting a detailed history of the gas container wagons can be shown by taking one example: 016S, former LSWR 17S, was built in 1883; its frame was condemned in 1926, and the cylinder moved to the frame of LSW luggage van No. 5065; in 1935 this frame was broken up and the cylinder moved to another one, the frame being renumbered 2007S and the cylinder 2072S. With double-cylinder wagons it was even more complex. There were some odd ones dotted about the numbering system, for example No. 468S, an LBSC cylinder on an LSW frame, converted in 1944 to a creosote wagon; Nos. 0550/1S which were SECR tanks on LSW frames. By 1945 all remaining gas lighting container wagons had been placed in a 2XXX series; two noted on bogie frames were Nos. 2052S and 2060S; apart from that, Nos. 2001S–2014S and 2083S–2100S were single tanks, 2035S–2080S double.

Examples of lettering noted: 02S 'Full to Exeter Queen Street, Empty to Eastleigh'; 015S 'Full to Salisbury, Empty to Clapham Junction'; 122S 'Full to Lancing, Empty to Brighton; 127S 'Full to Maze Hill, Empty to Rotherhithe Road'; 01070S 'Full' to Charing Cross, Empty to Rotherhithe Road'.

In the 1920s these vehicles could be seen at most large stations; for example one was usually in a short bay at the east end of Exeter Queen Street; this is not surprising when it is realised that in 1928 there were still 2298 gas-lit coaches and passenger vans on the SR, though this total was reduced each year. Gas lighting had been able to hold its own against electric train lighting due to the discovery about 1904 that incandescent gas mantles could be used in place of the bats-wing flame; it had been thought that they could not withstand the vibration. The mantles used much less gas than the open flame, and provided adequate light which the latter did not. The last gas-lit carriages ran in 1939. However the wagons continued in use, in some cases up to the early 1960s, for gas used in various workshops and depots. Some at Eastleigh are said to have been converted for carrying water. There must also have been a need for gas wherever restaurant cars were stored, until they were converted to Calor. It appears that some new tank wagons were created after 1950, Nos. 2101S–2133S, all on bogie frames, empty to Eastleigh or Rotherhithe Road.

Two LBSC Craven tenders used for water-carrying, photographed in 1901; that on the left is numbered 3.

O.J. Morris

RE-USE OF LOCOMOTIVE TENDERS

The use of tenders from scrapped engines as service stock goes back a long way, though in the earlier years many were found new engines. However, as time went on designs changed; for instance, when Stroudley's 'singles' were being scrapped, nobody would consider putting his tenders with their large inside-bearing wheels on to a Billinton engine. So they became in many cases 'sludge tenders'. The LBSC had set up a number of water-softening plants at big engine sheds from about 1910. A mixture of slaked lime and carbonate of soda was added to the water in a large tower, and insoluble solids fell to the bottom as a white sludge paste. The tenders were adapted by removing the rear tool-box and coal rails, fitting a buffered beam at the engine end, and placing large mud-holes in pairs on each side for 'mucking out'. Some of these tenders had to make quite long journeys; the Eastbourne sludge-tender was discharged at Three Bridges. These old Stroudleys gradually disappeared, around 1935; it was noted that Brighton shed was using an ex-Stirling tender, 0813S, similarly modified.

The most public place for a sludge tender was beneath the large water-tank at London Bridge, which could be examined from platform 10; LBSC No. 4 was there, painted up as 0988S in 1929, and later 501S, both Stroudleys. One was also kept at Victoria and several at New Cross Gate.

Another use was for the removal of waste products of gas-oil plants. Although some railways used coal gas for carriage lighting, most made their own gas from oil; the SECR had such a plant at Rotherhithe Road sidings. The process left a residue of tar; one of the very rare notes on Service stock in the early *Railway Magazine* appeared in 1910: 'old tender No. 141A of Beattie design has recently been converted into a travelling gas-tar tank, for use between Exmouth Junction and Farnham'. A number of these old Beattie tenders were noted at Eastleigh for scrapping in 1932: 0529S (LS11), 0534S (LS18), 0549S (LS19). Their place was taken by tenders off Adams engines: 0521S from E547, 457S from E0470, 599S from E566, this last being lettered 'When empty return to Wimbledon Gasworks'. Most had their coal-rail removed; no mud-holes were fitted. Beattie type 0524S (LS23) was based at Wimbledon also. All Beattie tenders had their centre axle removed, but this did not apply to other types.

Tenders were also used to carry drinking water; No. 526S was for 'Drinking Water Port Victoria' – this outpost by the estuary did not have its own supply; No. 423S, off B2X No. B207, was provided to supply workmen building the nearby Allhallows Branch in 1932. Sometimes tenders were pressed into service without repainting; that off Stirling 'O' class No. 286 stood in the siding at Lydd in Kent for some years in its SECR livery, until fitted with mud-holes and painted up as 0813S in about 1935. Similary the tender of No. 171 hung about at Ashford, from 1923 until 1928 when it emerged as 0818S. Ashford Laundry employed Stirling tenders Nos. 1054S –1057S; later No. DS1762–4 (Stirling) went to Exmouth Junction shed.

Two Adams tenders numbered 61384/5 were allocated in 1947 for carrying tar in the IOW; their tare weight was 11 tons and they were lettered to

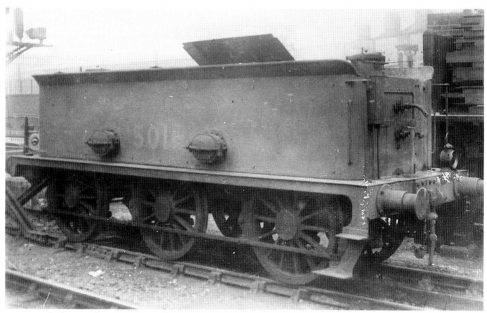

Sludge tender No. 501S, from a Stroudley engine, beneath the water-tank at London Bridge in April 1931; two mud-holes are fitted on both sides. *Author*

The tender off SER 'O' class 0–6–0 No. 286 was used as a water-carrier at Lydd, still in SECR livery; then numbered 0813S in 1936 as an oil tank, and later fitted with mud-holes for sludge carrying; here seen at Brighton about 1946. *Lens of Sutton*

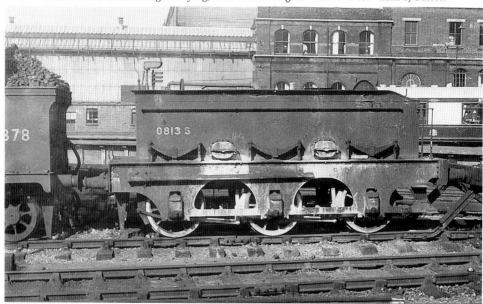

One of a pair of Adams LSWR tenders modified in 1947 to carry tar in the IOW, but returned to the mainland soon after. *Lens of Sutton*

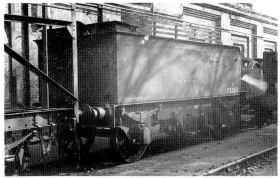

No. 0535S was a Beattie tender converted in 1931 to carry gas-oil at Eastleigh, and here carries the confusing messages 'Gas Works Only', the letter E for Western Section, and 'Ashford Works Yard Only'. *Lens of Sutton*

Ex-LBSC tender off 'B2X' class No. B207, as a water carrier numbered 423S at Allhallows in May 1932 containing drinking water for the workmen building the station. Behind is No. 0621S (SECR 21S) converted from an LCDR carriage of 1885 with an extra roof added. *Author*

A cigarette card in the 1936 series 'Railway Equipment' issued by Wills, showing the weed-killing train made up from two 'F' class and two 'B' class tenders, and ex-SECR double-ended guard's van No. 1110S (former SR 512 of 1900). *Author's Collection*

The frames of 'A12' 0–4–2 class LSWR engines were used for this set of weed-killing tank wagons of BR, close-coupled in pairs. DS463/460/462 are shown here; lettered 'CCE Department. For the use of weed-killing chemicals only'. *Lens of Sutton*

carry 17 tons. The resulting 11-ton axle loading was not liked, and after a period of limited use they were returned in 1949.

Tender frames were also used as crane match-trucks; one such No. 33SM (LSW 63S) was in use as a yard wagon at Eastleigh in 1932 though condemned in 1927. Another use was for three special brake vans for the 1 in 30 Folkestone Harbour incline, Nos. 55180–2, having half-length bodies and an open portion.

A new use came in 1931 with the first weed-killing train, tried out at East Grinstead; Adams tenders Nos. 572/3S, front-to-front, with nozzles worked by a guard leaning out of an attendant van (ex-LBSC goods brake vans Nos. 613/4S were used). In 1936 a larger train was built: Stirling 'F' class tenders 1038/9S, 'B' class 1040/1S. The sprays were mounted on a former double-ended SECR 6-wheeled passenger van No. 1110S (former SR 512), with windows cut in the end. Next year ex-SECR van No. 1234S was also so modified. A later train comprised converted SR Utility vans, the leading one with end windows, three pairs of tenders, and a 'pillbox' goods guards van (vans 55719/11 were converted to DS455/6). After nationalisation a train contained four BR tanks lettered 'CCE Dept. For use of weed-killing chemicals only', mounted on the frames of former 'A12' class engines, numbered DS 460–3.

There was a weed-killing train also in the IOW, using ex-IWC goods brake No. 17 (427S) and old tank wagons Nos. 422S and 443S. (*For details of later weed-killing trains, see Chapter 7.*)

Six tenders and two 1940 utility vans make up this later weed-killing train, which is being worked push-and-pull with a 'Q'class 0–6–0 propelling at Redgate Mill Junction in 1951.   *Lens of Sutton*

The 'Terrier' *Millwall* No. 38 had a strange career; transferred to the Loco. Dept, it was sold in 1918 to the War Department and shunted at Invergordon Docks in Scotland. Then in 1923 it was sold again, to the Shropshire & Montgomeryshire Railway, becoming their *Dido*; it was laid aside in 1932 but some parts later returned to the SR. *S.J. Rhodes*

Two 'E1' class 0−6−0T engines were used in locomotive depots, from 1909 to 1922, Nos. 99 and 111, returning to capital stock as 610/1; this could be either, photographed in June 1920. *H.C. Casserley*

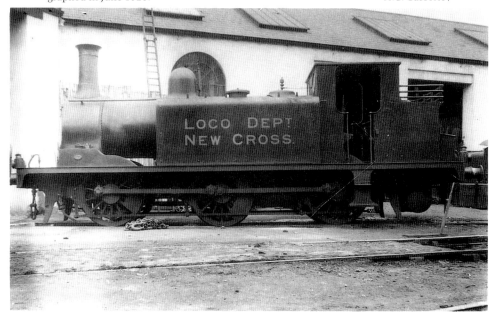

Chapter Five
Service Locomotives and Inspection Cars

From the very early years all railways had locomotives which were referred to as 'Ballast Engines', underpowered machines which could not be trusted in public use. The LSWR former a special stud of these, mostly second-hand, and put them in a different livery, named (with one exception) after well-known engineers and numbered in an Engineers Department series. In 1887 they were returned to capital stock as Nos. 01–015, but had gone a few years later, apart from *Scott* which was loaned to the Lee-on-the-Solent Railway. They were: 1. *Hawkshaw*, 2. *Brunel*, 3. *Stephenson*, 4. *Locke*, 5. *Smeaton*, 6. *Telford*, 7. *Fowler* (all G. England 2–4–0 built 1857 –64); 8. *Mina* (Walker 0–4–0T 1872); 9. *Harrison*, 10. *Bidder* (G. England 1862); 11. *Yolland*, 12. *Tyler* (R. Stephenson 0–6–0 1866); 13. *Rich*, 14. *Hutchinson* (R. Stephenson 2–4–0 1866); 15. *Scott* (G. England 1862 2–4 –0). In 1884 Nos. 2 and 3 were scrapped, being replaced by Nos. 147 and 148 from capital stock.

Nos. 9 and 10, although built in 1862 were purchased as unused in 1865; they were 'long-boiler' type 2–4–0s and ran in capital stock as Nos. 201/2 until 1872. In that year they were numbered 9 and 10 in the ED list; as only one engine is reported as being placed in that list before 1872, it must be assumed there were earlier engines allocated to 'ballast' work, scrapped by the 'eighties, and that the above list is only as it existed in 1887.

Scott had an interesting history; exhibited by its makers at the 1862 Exhibition, sold to the Somerset & Dorset Railway (No. 11), purchased by the LSWR in 1871, it was rebuilt in 1887 as a tank, renumbered 015 in 1895 and 21 in 1898, and put on the duplicate list in 1904 by having a bar under its number. At some date after 1898 it was loaned to the Lee-on-Solent Railway, but later returned to Nine Elms and was scrapped in 1909. For some of its early years it was stationed at Wimbledon p.w. depot.

After the last of its early ED stud was scrapped in 1891, the LSWR managed its service requirements with various small tank engines. These included *Pioneer*, a Manning, Wardle 0–4–0ST of 1879, which was purchased in 1891 and was used for shunting on the Waterloo & City 'tube' in its early years, later at Woking and Eastleigh. *Jessie* was a similar engine purchased in 1883; these two were numbered 407/8. The engines *Jumbo*, *Sambo* and *Bodmin*, which worked the Bodmin & Wadebridge branch when it was an isolated line, may also have been used in the works at times. In 1892 the LSWR bought Southampton Docks, and with it some small engines, which were later noted working at Eastleigh: No. 118 *Vulcan* (Vulcan Foundry 1878), *Bretwalda* (Hawthorn, LSWR 408); *Clausentum* (Hawthorn, Leslie 1890) numbered 457; *Ironside* (Hawthorn) numbered 458.

No. 457, 0457 from 1913, lasted until 1945; No. 458 survived to become BR 30458 as shed pilot at Guildford.

The LBSC allocated various small engines to duties at Brighton Works (and later Lancing Works after it was started up in 1907) and also major sheds. Their tanks carried 'Locomotive Department' but usually no number.

Vulcan was one of several engines taken over with the Southampton Docks which were used for shunting at Eastleigh Works; it was built by Vulcan Foundry in 1878; here seen at Eastleigh in April 1922.

H.C. Casserley

Ironside, built by Hawthorn in 1890, was one of the Southampton Docks Board engines bought by the LSWR and used as a shunter at Eastleigh; as No. EO458 she was Guildford shed shunter in the 1930s.   *Author's Collection*

Scott, a George England 2–4–0T of 1861, is seen here in LSWR Engineer's Department livery. Later she was loaned to the Lee-on-the-Solent Railway for passenger work.   *Author's Collection*

'Terrier' No. 377S had some 'outings'; she worked the Caterham Railway Centenary Special in 1956, and here in June the same year is working a Society Special to Kemp Town.
H.C. Casserley

No. DS238, a USA tank engine, shunting at Ashford after naming as *Wainwright*. The engine has now been on the Kent & East Sussex Railway for many years.
A.C. Ingram

The majority were 'A1' and 'A1X' class (Terriers) though 'E1' 0–6–0Ts Nos. 610 and 611 served until returning to capital stock in 1922. The 'Terriers' so used were:

638, former 38 *Millwall*; sold 1918 to Invergordon Dockyard, later *Dido* on Shropshire & Montgomeryshire Rly.

642, former 42 *Tulsehill*; at Battersea from 1919 to 1922.

380S, former 82 *Boxhill*; Service from 1932, reverted to capital stock as B682, preserved 1946 in LBSC livery.

680S, former 54 *Waddon* and SECR 751, SR A751, to Service 1932; to Eastleigh 1962, returned to LBSC livery, sent to Canada.

515S, former 50 *Whitechapel*; SR B650, to Lancing 1937, returned to capital stock as 32650 1953; presented to Sutton Borough Council 1964, later worked on KESR on loan.

377S, former 35 *Morden* and SR B635; to Service 1946, 1959 reverted to capital stock as 32635, but still in LBSC livery lettered Brighton Works (from 1947); withdrawn 1963.

The last two were 'A1X' class.

The SECR numbered its Service locos in with the capital stock, but after 1923 they were allotted S numbers:

225S 0–4–0ST Manning, Wardle 1881 SECR 313, sent 1925 to Meldon Quarries, Okehampton: withdrawn 1939.

234S 0–4–0T Neilson crane engine 1881, SECR 302, at Ashford and later Stewarts Lane, to capital stock as 1302, 1938: withdrawn 1949.

235S 0–4–0T Neilson crane engine 1896, SECR 409, at Ashford, withdrawn 1935.

236S 0–6–0T Manning, Wardle 1890. SECR 353; did not carry new number, withdrawn at Ashford 1929, scrapped 1932.

Other SR service locomotives were:

500S, 0–6–0T LCDR 'T' class, SECR No. 607, to Meldon Quarry 1938, withdrawn 1949.

77S 0–4–0T LSWR, SR 0745, to Redbridge sleeper depot 1927, withdrawn 1959.

700S 0–4–2T LBSCR 'D1' class, SR 2244 withdrawn 1949.

701S 0–4–2T LBSCR 'D1' class, SR 2284, to Nine Elms 1947, adapted for oil-pumping, withdrawn 1951.

Departmental transfers during the British Rail period included:

DS3152 'G6' class 0–6–0T 30272 to Meldon Quarry 1949.

DS681 'A1x' class 0–6–0T 32659, 1953, withdrawn 1963.

DS682, 'G6' class 0–6–0T 30238, 1960, withdrawn 1962.

DS233 'USA' class 0–6–0T 30061, 1962, to Redbridge, withdrawn 1967.

DS234 'USA' class 0–6–0T 30062, 1962, to Meldon Qy, withdrawn 1967.

DS235 'USA' class 0–6–0T 30066, 1963, to Lancing, withdrawn 1965.

DS236 'USA' class 0–6–0T 30074, 1963, to Lancing, withdrawn 1965.

DS237 'USA' class 0–6–0T 30065, 1963, to Ashford, withdrawn 1967, to KESR.

DS238 'USA' class 0–6–0T 30070, 1963, to Ashford, withdrawn 1967, to KESR.

DS239 'C' class 0–6–0 31592 withdrawn 1966, to private owner, at Bluebell.

DS240 'C' class 0–6–0 31272 to stationary boiler, Ashford, 1965.

DS237 named *Maunsell*, DS238 *Wainwright*.

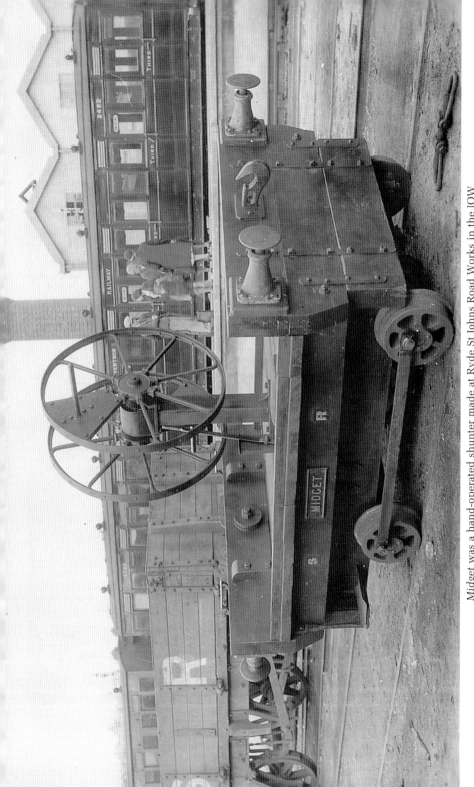

Midget was a hand-operated shunter made at Ryde St Johns Road Works in the IOW and used from 1929 to 1938.

F. Moore

This 'Terrier', No. 680S here at Brighton Works in January 1933, ended up in Canada. Formerly 54 *Waddon* it was sold to the SECR in 1904. It was transferred to Central Section service stock in 1932. In 1962 it went to Eastleigh to be put back into LBSC livery and was then shipped to Canada for preservation.   *Author*

Mr Drummond's private runabout, built in 1899 as LSWR 733, later SR 58S, with single driving wheel 5 ft 7 in., seen here at Southampton Docks where it ran private parties around the new workings in 1933–4. It was scrapped in 1940.   *L.T. Catchpole*

The end of steam at Ashford saw DS240 taken off boiler duties and DS239 being prepared for preservation. DS237/8 were noted at Tonbridge in March 1968 on their way to a new life on the KESR.

Small petrol or diesel engines were used in some depots. At Broad Clyst sleeper depot there was a motorised carriage bogie with home-made body, carrying the probably unofficial number 49. In the same depot there was DS169, a Ruston & Hornsby engine with only 5½ ft wheelbase. 1173S was a Drewry diesel loco built in 1946 and purchased in 1948; it worked at Hither Green and was later numbered D2341. At Eastleigh Carriage Works there were petrol loco No. 343S and Fowler 0–4–0D 600S; and at Southampton Docks diesel 400S.

In the Isle of Wight there was a 'locomotive' with a name but no number; called Midget, it was built at Ryde St Johns Road, a small four-coupled trolley shunter powered by two capstan wheels mounted on its deck; it was for moving boilers on flats and so on, but was said to be capable of moving a bogie carriage. It was built in 1929 and laid aside some ten years later. A French Secamfer diesel-hydraulic 0–4–0 built in 1965 was sent to Woking in 1967 carrying its French number 2332S though allotted DS209.

In 1905 the LBSC had purchased two Dick, Kerr petrol railcars, running on four wheels but of considerable length. One was designated an inspection saloon in 1914 (the other was unserviceable) but in 1916 both were handed over to the electrical department, which fitted roof platforms and used them for repairs to overhead wiring; they were stationed at Peckham Rye depot. O.J. Morris reported that they were still there 'some time after the Overhead had gone'; they were allotted numbers 344/5S.

Combined engines and saloons for inspection purposes were not common, but the Southern companies had two. There was the LBSCR Inspector 2–4–2T; this had started life as a Sharp, Stewart 2–4–0T on the Kensington branch, and was rebuilt and renamed twice as Kemp Town and Hayling Island to work on those branches. In 1889 William Stroudley lengthened the frame and added a trailing axle, with a small saloon over it, close to the track. It was given over to the chief PW Inspector, Mr Lomes, but he does not seem to have used it much; it was reported in 1899 as having been in the paint shop at Shoreham Road, Brighton, 'for some years' and was scrapped soon after.

Dugald Drummond of the LSWR built a rather larger machine, a 4–2–4T, with a good-sized saloon at the rear, and used it to travel from his Surbiton home to all parts of the system. Built in 1899, and numbered 733, it does not seem to have been used in the early years of the SR, but was renumbered 58S and in the early thirties carried VIPs around the new Southampton Docks, paired with ex-SECR 6-wheeled saloon No. 0824S.

INSPECTION SALOONS

LSWR 6-wheel saloon No. 9, later 09, was used for inspection purposes and renumbered 073S by the SR, although it remained in pre-grouping livery until 1932. It was originally open-ended; the roof seems to have been

One of two Neilson crane engines owned by the SER; No. 302, (1881) later A234S left Ashford for Brighton about 1936, and two years later went to Longhedge, where some rebuilding took place; renumbered 1302; it was not withdrawn until 1949. Seen here at Brighton, 22nd August, 1936.

H.C. Casserley

A1x 'Terrier' No. 377S was originally No. 35 *Morden*, then B635, moved to service work in 1937 and in 1947 painted in LBSC livery; restored to capital stock as 32635 about 1960 but retained LBSC livery; withdrawn in 1962.   *O.J. Morris*

No. 515S was an A1x class, former 50 *Whitechapel*, SR B650, transferred to Lancing Works in 1937; in 1953 it returned to BR as 32650, and was later presented to Sutton Borough Council for preservation in 1964, and works now on the K&ESR.
L.W. Perkins

The former rail-motor engine E0745 went to Redbridge Sleeper Depot in 1927 as 77S, and stayed there until withdrawal; here seen in May 1957. *H.C. Casserley*

A 'G6' class 0–6–0T, No. 30272, was transferred in 1949 to Meldon Quarry, Okehampton, as DS3152; here seen in August 1954 working the workmen's train.
H.C. Casserley

A PETROL-DRIVEN RAILWAY INSPECTION CAR

The first 'Sheffield' petrol-driven inspection car in England for railway work was officially tested on November 23. Mr Robert W.A. Brewer, AMICE, AMIME, of London, who has for a number of years been engaged in expert oil-engine and motor-car work, was asked by the makers to conduct the trials.

Portions of the South-Western Railway Company's line in the vicinity of Exeter were selected by Mr Grainger, superintendent of the permanent way for the company, who was a passenger on the car, together with Mr O.S. Wilson, European manager for the makers, Messrs Fairbanks, Morse, and Co., Chicago.

The trials lasted from 10 am till 3 pm, the results being most satisfactory. A speed of 30 miles per hour was maintained on the level, with eight passengers; gradients of 1 in 100 with eight, 1 in 50 with five, and 1 in 37 on a curve with three passengers were successfully negotiated from a standing start.

The car tested, of which we annex an engraving, was of 6 horse-power, having two water-cooled cylinders, the connecting-rods driving direct on the rear wheels. Automatic reversing gear is also fitted. The total weight of the car is 520 lb.

The South-Western Railway Company are taking the lead in the adoption of this car, which is a great improvement on anything at present in use for this purpose.

This cutting from *Engineering* of 28th November, 1902 announces the first trials, on the LSWR, of a motor inspection trolley. The lower photograph shows a similar but later car on an LBSC branch line.   *Author's Collection*

longer than the body, as the ends were 'stepped' when closed in. There was as short caboose on the roof; the vehicle was withdrawn in 1941. A larger saloon, running on 'American' bogies, was built in 1885; the LSWR numbered it 21S in 1895, and the SR made it 1S. The roof was extremely cluttered; towards the 'kitchen' end there was a short caboose, then three gas cylinders side by side, and beyond them a square water-tank with ribbed sides. In a 1950 rebuild the caboose was removed and the cylinders spaced out along the roof; it was also reframed on later bogies and lost its full length running board. Shortly after, the kitchen was converted to Calor gas and the ugly gas cylinders went. The saloon had end doors and drop-plates. It served in Kent for driver-training from 1958 to 1961 and was withdrawn in 1963.

Stroudley designed a bogie saloon for Directors in 1889, numbered 72; the open verandah ends were closed in by Billinton, and it later became SR saloon No. 7969, being withdrawn in 1930. A later saloon, built in 1914 and numbered 60, was a twelve-wheeler, which became SR 291S, and is now on the Bluebell Railway.

A 6-wheeled saloon built by the SER in 1886 appeared in the Register as inspection saloon No. 195S 'fitted detaching arrangements', so presumably a slip-coach; from 1926 it ran as public saloon 1st brake No. 7765.

In 1946 the Southern Railway built a sleeping car for the use of its top management, principally Mr Bulleid. It was numbered 100S and ran with generator van 97S (ex-SECR LV 1987) and two dining cars 98S (ex-7940) and 99S (ex-7943) and a 'nondescript' brake coach 444S (ex-4444). The car had a plywood body, 64½ ft long, with a single centre door and six windows high up the sides. There were twelve berths. Its existence was kept fairly quiet; it was housed at Stewarts Lane and only noted out on the road once. The sleeping car itself was burnt at Lancing in 1956.

In 1962 a new Guards Instruction Saloon TDS70155 was made from a Hastings line composite No. 5600; it was often teamed with a class 71 electric locomotive, and carried a headcode in a box below the front windows at the control end. This coach was later moved to the K&ESR.

Inspection Saloon TDM395280 had been converted in 1958, from ex-LMS carriage stock, and had the low front windows characteristic of Derby-built saloons; it was noted on the SR, mainly in the West, but also at Clapham Junction.

A 1970 General Manager's Saloon, TDB975025 was formed from a Hastings demu set buffet car, and was used as a Royal Saloon for the honeymoon journey of the Prince of Wales in July 1981.

For lower management, the petrol engine provided a means of inexpensive personal transport. The LSWR took the lead in November 1902, when Mr Grainger, the PW superintendent, tried out a motor trolley called the 'Sheffield', from the USA. It had two cylinders driving the rear axle direct and carrying eight passengers. This would have needed push-starting and must have been terrifying.

In 1906 the LBSC acquired a British-built car, seating four, labelled 'Engineers Inspection Car, Northern Division', and based at Fairfield depot, East Croydon. This was replaced in 1915 with a Drewry/Baguley car (later SR

Two views of the bogie electric locomotive No. 74S, which was used for many years as a shunter at Durnsford Road power station and electric train depot, Wimbledon and was withdrawn in 1969.   *R.C. Riley*

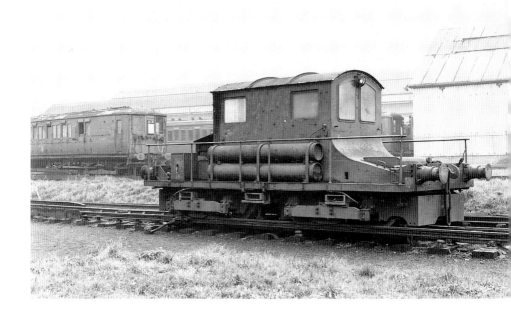

This Alldays & Onions car of 1906 was lettered 'LB & SCR Inspectors Car Northern Division' and was based at Croydon. The headboard it is carrying was traditionally used for inspection cars, but from 1900–1908 was also carried by all trains running via the Quarry Line deviation.

Author's Collection

Inspection saloon No. 073S (LSWR No. 9 ot 1877) seen here at Paddock Wood in August 1932, shortly after repainting from pre-grouping livery.   *Author*

The LSWR bogie inspection saloon built in 1885, at Faversham for driver-training in 1959, having lost the 'caboose' over the kitchen area and the three gas-tanks it had carried on the roof.   *R.C. Riley*

Stroudley designed this bogie Directors' saloon in 1889, numbered 72; it was later rebuilt by Billinton with enclosed ends and returned to capital stock, becoming SR 7969, withdrawn in 1930. *Lens of Sutton*

The LBSC had this twelve-wheeled saloon built for it by Billinton in 1914, numbered 60. It became SR 291S. It is here at Stewarts Lane in May 1958; it was later taken over by the Bluebell Railway. *R.C. Riley*

In 1946 the SR built a sleeping car for the use of its Directors, numbered 100S. Its plywood body contained twelve sleeping berths, and it ran with various ancillary vehicles (*see text*). *Lens of Sutton*

346S), which though quite small, had a three-door body. It was seen in many parts of the SR after Grouping, lastly allocated to Redhill in 1954. In LBSC days the cars, which had five lamp-irons, carried route head-codes, though sometimes it seems that the disc with horizontal stripes, from 1900 used as the 'Quarry Line' board, was used regardless. The Baguley car weighed 1 ton 12 cwt., had a 20 hp 4 cylinder engine, and was reputedly able to run at 31 mph.

After Grouping, the Drewry railcar on the Isle of Wight, which the Freshwater, Yarmouth & Newport Railway had used as a 'boat Train' from Newport to Yarmouth, was designated an inspection car, No. 437S, but was withdrawn in 1927. Smaller motorised 'Wickham' trolleys for PW gangs became common on the SR; after nationalisation some more powerful trolleys were provided, and light 4-door trailers (DS53 was one) attached when required. The trailers had five lamp-irons and could be run push-pull.

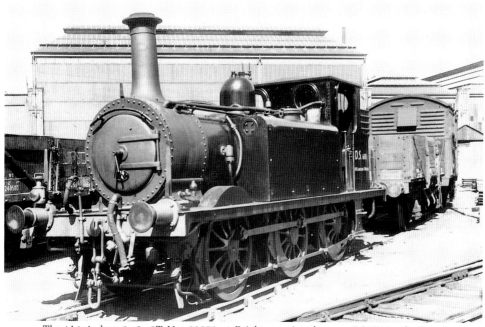

The 'A1x' class 0–6–0T No. 32659 at Brighton painted up as DS681 in the latest livery with small numerals for Lancing Works, September 1953.   R.C. Riley

Chapter Six
Electric Service Stock

The LSWR acquired the first electric 'service vehicle' in 1898, a small Siemens 4-wheeled locomotive for shunting stock on its Waterloo & City 'tube' line. This was withdrawn in 1969 and later went to York Museum. It had a dropped frame at the driving end, a short body of 'tube' style, and a small platform at the rear end, which at any rate latterly carried normal height buffing gear. It was numbered 75S in SR days.

In 1899 a bogie electric locomotive, later SR 74S, was acquired from Dick, Kerr; its early use is uncertain, but on the electrification of some LSWR suburban lines, in 1915, it was employed at the depot and power station at Durnsford Road, Wimbledon, and remained there for more than 40 years. It had a narrow iron body in the centre (with a door on one side only) which curved down to platforms at each end; a footplate with stanchions was fitted on both sides. It is believed that it remained after the power station closed in 1958 and was used occasionally until 1965.

The use by the LBSC and SR of two former petrol railcars for servicing overhead wiring has been mentioned in the previous chapter.

For the massive electrification projects of 1926 onwards, the SR used conventional service stock, though some was lettered for electrification work, including stores vans, riding vans, and open wagons modified for cable-laying. The use of surplus electric stock for service purposes was forced by the realisation after the War that the delays caused in winter by icing of the live rails could not continue. In 1945 some coaches from the non-motored two-coach trailer sets of LBSC origin were fitted with tanks to contain de-icing fluid, and nozzles on booms attached to the bogie; these worked between two 3-SUB sets during the nights; Nos. 351S–356S were noted, also some later conversions, DS396–399; most were located at Selhurst.

Some two-coach de-icing sets were made up in 1960 using motor coaches from the 1925 Met-Vick steel-panelled stock; they were given unit numbers S93–101, later numbered 012–020; all were withdrawn in 1977–81.

There were also some 'tractor units', coaches from former LBSC-bodied DCE sets, used to ferry trailer coaches to Eastleigh: DS347/8 were from former 3-SUB unit 1764; they were withdrawn in 1963.

In 1956 an Instructional train was made up from the original coaches of 3-SUB unit 1782 (later 4-SUB 4579), being reframed and lengthened LSW coaches. This train numbered S10 (later 053), coaches DS40–2, was vestibuled and had in its first coach a motorman's and guard's compartment and a lecture and projection room; the second contained samples of all kinds of power control equipment; the third was devoted to power collection, lighting and heating equipment, and also had a motorman's compartment.

In 1960 a 4SUB trailer coach No. 10400 was converted to a de-icing coach, ADS 70087, booms for spray nozzles being fitted to both bogies. Third-rail icing problems had been causing chaos on two or three days each winter since the 1920s. When only inner London lines were electrified and there

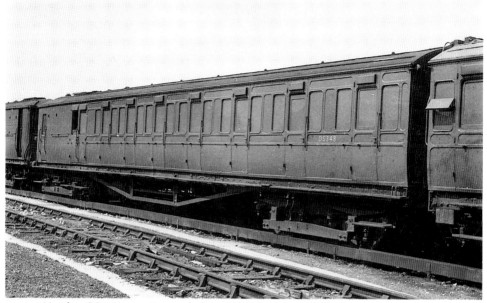

Number DS348, a motor-coach from LBSC-bodied 4-SUB unit 1764, used to ferry trailer coaches to Micheldever or Eastleigh; photographed in May 1963.   R.C. Riley

De-icing coach DS399, formerly 9089 in an electric 2-car trailer unit, about 1949.
Lens of Sutton

was a plentiful supply of steam engines to be pressed into service to assist, it was fairly easily overcome. As the third rail extended further into the Home Counties the confusion was greater, as yard shunters from Gillingham or Brighton found themselves unexpectedly at the head of a semi-fast at a London terminus. By 1967 as the end of steam approached, very serious thought was given to the position which might arise in the coming winter with trains stranded without hope of rescue. British Rail announced that 15 de-icing trains would be available next winter, with improved de-icing fluid. From now on, what had been a rather small-scale *ad hoc* exercise was to be an increasingly sophisticated and expensive part of the Region's non-revenue activities.

As it happened, 1968 offered a good example of icing chaos in spite of the 15 trains; this was on Boxing Day, and perhaps few workers could be mustered on Christmas Day evening. Today of course it would not matter, as scarcely any trains run on Boxing Day.

In the Isle of Wight, after more recent LTE stock had arrived, some of the 1923–7 stock was retained to be used for de-icing purposes.

The de-icing sets originally carried low numbers where the former set number had been, and later an S prefix. In 1971 an 0XX series was started for these and continued in use, though some were becoming in poor condition by the late 1960s, and a new series was begun, using 2HAL motor coaches, for de-icing trains. For the autumn of 1974, sets 001/2 were converted to

De-icing set No. 95, made up from original 3-SUB stock (coaches 8453/4) seen here at Knights Hill in September 1960.   R.C. Riley

An Instruction Train was made up in 1956 using former LSW-bodied 3-SUB set 1782; shown here is DS41, the coach devoted to a display of various types of power equipment. *Lens of Sutton*

This de-icing van, No. DS70086, is one of several designed to work between service motor coaches, and made from 'Augmentation' 4-SUB trailers in the 1970s. *Lens of Sutton*

water-cannon sets for leaf-clearing; they were loco-hauled. The coaches were considerably modified; No. 002 had only a driver's door, a double door, and two single doors left. Heavy leaf-fall was of course not a new phenomenon in the leafy cuttings, but had not mattered much in steam days. With demus and emus there was serious wheelspin and skidding, causing wheel-flats, which kept far too many sets in the shops. The water-cannons were not entirely effective, and in 1981 there was a change to a substance called Sandite, which had a gelatinous content and stuck to the rail surface.

The later de-icing sets were devised so that the spray switched itself on when it met the live rail, and off when it left it; this meant no wasted spray when the live rail changed sides.

In 1968 two-coach sets 001/2 were made up from HAL/LAV stock, and in 1977–9 sets 003–012 were made from two coaches each of 4SUB stock. These were all de-icing or Sandite sets. No. 013 was made from 4SUB motors in 1982, and Nos. 015/16 from 4EPB motors in 1982. Numbers 018/9 were stores units from 2HAP stock; 021 was a tractor unit for ferrying coaches between depots; 022/3 from 2HAL stock and 024 from 4SUB were Stores and Test sets, dated 1970 and 1973 respectively.

Sets 032–4 were from 4CAP stock, the last being intended to work with single coach ADB977634 at Ramsgate. The following have also been noted:

050   Tractor unit
051   From LNW (NL line) electrics, research unit, DB975027–9. Withdrawn 1972.
052   From LNW (NL line) electrics, stores unit, DB975030–2. Withdrawn 1970.
053   Renumbering of former instruction unit S10 of 1956
054   From 2HAP Service Unit, DB(77207/8)
055   Instruction unit from set 4367, 1974
056   Test Unit from PEP set 4001 1979
057   Test Unit from PEP set 4002 1980
061   Stores unit from 2HAL 1970
062   'Liquid Delivery Unit' from Tyneside EPB motors
063   Stores unit from 2HAL
064   Stores unit
065   Stores unit
066   Stores unit
067   Sandite set (3 coaches) from Hastings set 203001
068   Sandite set from 207 cl. used with de-icer coach ADB977696
080   Test train from 4CEP stock
081   Traction power test train from 4CEP stock

This is not a definitive list, as some numbers have been changed and some formations altered.

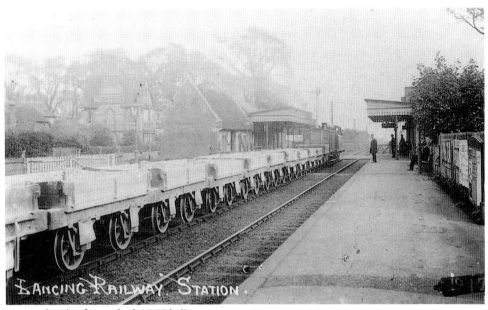

A train of two-plank LBSC ballast wagons at Lancing about 1920. *Lens of Sutton*

Ex-LBSC three-plank ballast wagon No. 62634, still fitted with dumb buffers, at Hoo Junction p.w. sidings on 20th September, 1931. *Author*

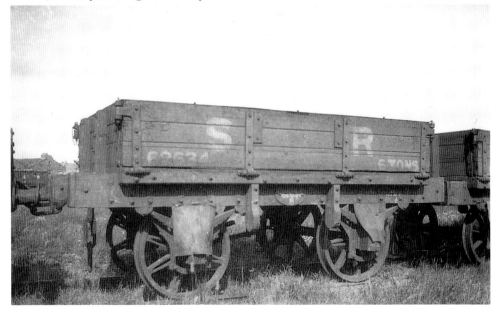

Chapter Seven
Track Maintenance Stock and Cranes

At the time of Grouping, a 'ballast train' implied about 20 two- or three-plank drop-side 6-ton wagons with a riding van or brake van at each end. On the SECR the latter would be old carriages, or on the LBSC purpose-built riding/brake vans, some six-wheeled. The LSWR had already obtained some up to date equipment for working ballast from its huge Meldon Quarry, but the other lines used mainly primitive stock, mostly with dumb buffers, and squares of canvas fixed over the journals to keep stone dust out.

The term 'ballast' originally referred to anything that might be put into a ship's hold when it was sailing 'in ballast', that is without cargo, to steady it. Thus some of the locations at which early SER ballast trains had regular workings, such as between Star Bridge and Coulsdon, between Gravesend and Higham, and at Abbotts Cliff were of chalky soil, no use for ballasting track but used for making embankments when the local cuttings did not provide enough 'spoil'. There were other 'ballast holes' of the right sort; the SER obtained much of its ballast from an area of pebbles at Dungeness which it had purchased; the LBSC took some via a 2½ mile siding to the large 'Shingles' area east of Eastbourne. Ballast trains mostly remained made up for some time, being parked when not required at locations other than regular sidings; the SECR used the big rubbish dump near Lee Junction, later occupied by Hither Green loco shed.

Under the old Companies most work was done at night. However the SER had specific instructions to be followed by ballast train crews and station staff for day-time working, some of which must surely not have been honoured, such as that requiring that 'the running of a ballast train must be announced to the Line by Special Board or Tail Lamp on the previous Ordinary Train'. Rule 7 stated that no ballast train must stop or unload between stations (either on a 'road siding' or the main line) without first stopping and giving notice at the station on either side. It must be assumed that one of these could be notified by telegraph of the train's arrival at the other. No ballast train was allowed to call at a station which was closed at night without opening it up and staffing the signal box. The only special instruction was that ballast trains working between Tonbridge and Tunbridge Wells had to have an extra brake van; Tonbridge was allocated 'No. 2 Ballast Train'.

In SR days every effort was made to avoid closing lines for PW work, and there was not a large gap between the last and first passenger train on many lines. If relaying was to be done, usually the new rails and chaired sleepers would be dumped by the trackside on one night, next night the spent ballast would be shovelled out and new track laid; then it would be left under a severe speed restriction until another night when new ballasting and fettling would be done. The rails were carried on 60 ft bogie flats with removable side stanchions and chains; sometimes a crane would go with them, but the gangs were large enough to carry rails by using the pincer-type carriers, six or eight persons to a rail.

A standard 40-ton SR ballast wagon, bottom-discharging and vacuum braked, No. 62012. *Lens of Sutton*

A train of ballast leaving Meldon Quarries, Okehampton, in 1933. *L.T. Catchpole*

A steel bottom-discharging ballast wagon built for the LBSCR by Hurst Nelson in 1922.

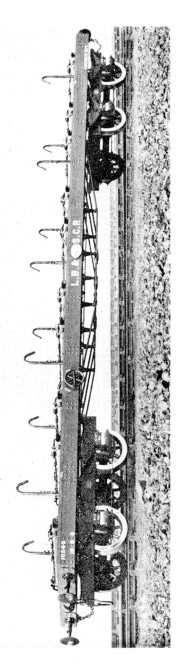

This type of rail wagon was introduced on the LBSCR in 1902; the stanchions were removable for loading and unloading.

Courtesy Locomotive Magazine

In early SR days most of the rails were sent by sea and landed at Anger-stein's Wharf (Greenwich), or Highbridge Wharf (S&DJR), although the latter could handle only about 180 tons at a time, in railway boats. At Angerstein's, the 60 ft rails had a few 'shorts' from 14 ft to 40 ft mixed in, to make a delivery by rail of some 160 tons; these shorts were used to equalise curves or make crossings. Near the point of use, most of the 'shorts' would be taken off to the nearest ED depot for making into points material. The rest would be left on the flat-wagon in most cases, to avoid handling twice, though some stocks were built up at PW depots. The chairs were mostly sent by sea to Angerstein's or to Redbridge Sleeper Depot. Sleepers were shipped direct to Redbridge for creosoting, though it did not have the capacity to serve the whole SR and some pressure creosoting was done by contractors. The annual purchase at that time was about 30,000 tons of rail, 11,000 chairs and 400,000 sleepers, though an experiment with steel sleepers was going on and 2,500 were used in 1931.

Of the old Companies, the SECR numbered ballast wagons in with others, the other two put them mostly in a duplicate series, though the LBSC painted their ballast brakes with large letters 'Ballast' and the number equally large. The SR decided to have an 'ED' number series, starting after the normal brake van numbers, and this included ballast wagons, rail flats, and brake or riding vans. The cranes were of course in the normal 'S' series. As has been stated, the Eastern Section used some old carriages as ED brakes, ex-LCD 4-wheel 3rd brakes and latterly various goods brake vans. There were also a few purpose-built old SER riding vans; these had outside body-framing and were similar in style (though longer) to the old 10-ton goods brakes. There was a guard's compartment at one end, with screw brake, and a saloon with benches around the sides and a stove and table in the middle. Some of these were in fact not very old; Nos. 62501–11 were built by MCW in 1900 to the 1865 design.

Some modern LBSC ballast brakes were numbered 62823–39; 62840–56 were former LBSC goods brakes transferred to ballast work. There was a batch of ex-LSWR ballast brakes. Nos. 61912–44. An example, No. 61913 marked 'return to Eardley Sidings', was a 15-ton 4-wheeled van having a door at one end, two side-windows, and also two windows and a ventilator at the non-door end.

In 1927 there was a requirement for further ballast train riding vans on the Eastern Section, and four were found from ex-SECR 'cyphered' coach sets recently in use as either hoppers' or workmen's stock, Nos. 02, 07, and 010; ED 62524/6 were 4-wheeled thirds, and ED 62525/7 4-wheeled 3rd brakes still oil-lit.

The Western Section used bogie hopper ballast wagons with bottom dis-charging and from the early thirties this type was also used on other sec-tions. They were 32 ft long, $17\frac{1}{4}$ tons tare, carrying 32 cubic yards. The brake vans used had 'ploughs', curved steel plates lowered to within one inch of rail level by gear inside the van, to spread ballast as it discharged. These vans were piped but not vacuum-braked.

By 1932 nearly 100,000 tons of ballast per year was being taken out of

E.D. YARD. WIMBLEDON.

A track maintenance crew joining a train in the Wimbledon p.w. depot about 1930; the 24 ft ex-LSW brake van No. 55917 was later numbered in ED stock. The engine is a 'T' class ex-LCDR 0–6–0T, a very rare visitor to the Western Section, and probably here on loan for the construction of the Wimbledon–Sutton line.

Lens of Sutton

An ex-SECR ballast train riding van at Hoo Junction in September 1931; this had a brake compartment at the left hand end, and a door from that into a saloon with stove and table and seats round the sides and end, accommodation for about 20 men.

Author

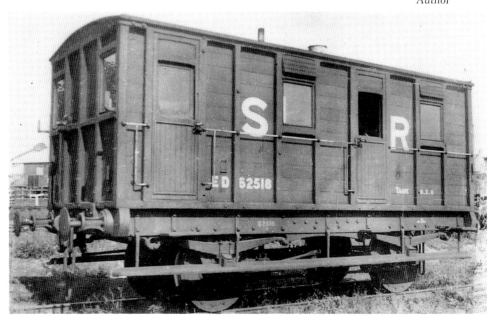

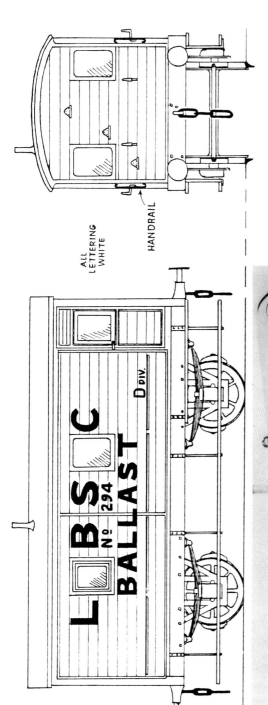

ALL LETTERING WHITE

HANDRAIL

0 1 2 3 4 5 6 FEET

LBSC ballast brake No. 294 was noted still in old livery in 1929, but later that year was painted up as SR ED 62833.

David Gould

LBSC ballast brake van No. 327.

Lens of Sutton

Meldon Quarry. Four times a week a train of ten 40-ton bogie hopper wagons left for one or other of the Sections, the actual work being done at night; the *Southern Railway Magazine* claimed that 400 tons of ballast could be dropped and spread in half an hour. There were special instructions in the 1934 Appendix to Working Time Tables for the movement of these heavy vacuum-braked trains through Exeter:

> Vacuum-fitted stone trains. – An Assistant engine must be provided at the rear of all up stone trains composed of vacuum stock as between Exeter St David's and Exeter Central.
>
> Stone trains composed of more than seven loaded large hopper wagons and van (vacuum fitted stock) may, if necessary, be assisted by two bank engines at the rear from Exeter St David's to Exeter Central.
>
> In the case of stone trains for Exeter Central or stations beyond with a load exceeding seven large vacuum fitted hopper wagons and van, requiring assistance by two bank engines at the rear, a telephonic advice must be sent from Okehampton to the Locomotive Foreman at Exeter Central, or to the Locomotive Foreman at Exmouth Junction and the Signalman at Exeter Central 'B' box, as the case may be, giving the time of departure and particulars of the load.
>
> The vacuum brake connection of bank engines attached to the rear and assisting stone trains composed of vacuum fitted hopper wagons from Exeter St David's to Exeter Central must be connected with the last vehicle so that the vacuum brake may be complete throughout the train, and the Guard will be responsible for seeing that this is done and the vacuum brake is in good working order before the train leaves Exeter St David's.
>
> In the case of a stone train composed of vacuum fitted hopper wagons requiring two bank engines in the rear, the Driver must give one short and two long whistles when passing Exeter St David's Middle signal box situated at Red Cow crossing.

Special rules also covered the movement of work trains to and from Angerstein's Wharf, the junction for which was between Blackheath Tunnel and Charlton:

> Drivers must enter the yard with extreme caution, and be prepared to bring their trains to a stand immediately they are signalled to do so. Brake vans must not be loose shunted off the trains when entering the yard.
>
> Guards of ballast trains, immediately on arrival at Angerstein Wharf home signal, must communicate with the wharf Shunter, and must not enter any siding without authority.
>
> Materials trains. – The Engineer's department Storekeeper at Angerstein Works will give 48 hours' notice to the London East Divisional Superintendent when these trains are required to run. The application will state the date, proposed time of departure from Angerstein Wharf, destination and class of material to be conveyed. The Engineer's department Storekeeper will, at the same time, advise the Goods Agent at Angerstein Wharf and the Divisional Engineer concerned of the arrangements which are being made.
>
> When the empty wagons forming these material trains are returned to Angerstein Wharf by special train and booked to arrive between 5.0 am on Sundays and 5.0 am on Mondays, the Goods Agent will arrange for a Shunter to be on duty to receive the trains.

Another proviso was that the 20-ton ballast wagons on the Central Section

An ex-LBSC ballast brake in SR livery at Merstham in 1929; it is lettered 'D Div' over the number (62839) and the letter B below the numer repeated on the sole bar.   *J.R.N. Stone*

A Western Section p.w. mess van No. DS61922, a former LSWR goods brake, at Brockenhurst in September 1953.
                         R.C. Riley

A 25 ft brake van modified as a riding van No. 62841, lettered 'Return to Hither Green Pre-Assembly dept, with crane No. 1579S. This brake is not to be detached'.   *Lens of Sutton*

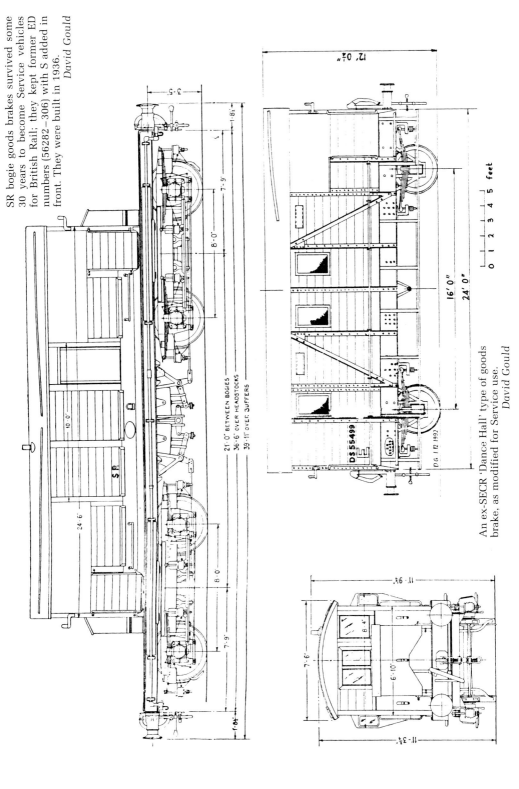

SR bogie goods brakes survived some 30 years to become Service vehicles for British Rail; they kept former ED numbers (56282–306) with S added in front. They were built in 1936.

David Gould

21'0" BETWEEN BOGIES
36'6" OVER HEADSTOCKS
39'11" OVER BUFFERS

3·5'
1·8'
7·9'
8·0'
10'0'
S R
24·6'
8·0'
7·9'
1·0'

DS55499

D.G 1 12 1992

12'0¾"

16'0"
24'0"

0 1 2 3 4 5 feet

An ex-SECR 'Dance Hall' type of goods brake, as modified for Service use.

David Gould

11'9¼"
8'4"
7'6"
6'10"
11'3¼"

must not be loose-shunted; this was because of 'the large number of turns on the brake wheel required'.

In the late 1930s, a new feature of work trains was the inclusion of an i.c. crawler-excavator on a low-loader. For the big landslide at Abbotts Cliff near Dover in November 1939, three of the largest excavators that could be got through the tunnels were sent in. Six months later when there were slips at Star Lane, Coulsdon, on both routes, a crawler was sent in working with the train on the Redhill line by night and on the 'Quarry' line by day.

The final phase began in BR days, when it became customary to send the gangs to relaying jobs in railway-owned road vehicles, thus cutting out the riding vans. By this time mechanical tamping machines had been introduced, many of which were self-propelling, and they were to be seen in various sidings from which they would move out when 'occupation' was obtained. The introduction of long-welded rail called for new types of bolster wagon; there was a world of difference between the ballast train of 50 years ago, clattering out at dead of night with its tiny wagons and old coaches, intent on completing the job before the first train was due next morning, and the present modern sophisticated engineering gear which is brought on to the site at a time more convenient to the workforce, and 'protected' by the cancellation of all services for two or three whole weekends.

In spite of the profusion of ballast brakes taken over at Grouping, and the conversion of some goods brakes to this job, the SR decided to build some new 20-ton vans in 1932 (ED 62030–32) copying an SECR design of which only one was built (ED62523). They were 25 ft long with an 18 ft wheelbase and ploughs within the wheelbase. A further batch (ED62857–64) was added in 1948. Many are still in use, some painted with the word 'Shark', which is applied to BR vans fitted with spreading ploughs.

In 1953 ten of the 'dance-hall' type of SECR goods brakes were converted for ED use; these were so-called from the great length of the body compared with the old standard SECR 10-tonners. The conversion involved sheeting over one end balcony and adding three side-windows. They kept their former numbers (55476/82/86/89/92–4/99, 502/8), with DS in front. Many unconverted ones were also used on ballast work, as was the 'pill-box' type van, named so because its short body sat in the middle of a frame the same length as the 'dance-hall'.

Another type seen on track maintenance work after goods brakes had been phased out in the 1970s was the Maunsell bogie type. The early ones had been rebuilds of LBSC elevated-electric motors, but two batches of straight-sided van were introduced later, and from the 1936 batch (56282–306) nine were still working in 1984/5 on SR track trains, while nine had been sent to other Regions on similar work; all kept their original numbers.

In the 1940s some ballast brakes were painted up with their precise use; for example 62842 was for ARP use; 62843/7 were each painted with the number of the crane they worked with; 62840 with crane No. 57 Beddington Lane.

When in the 1960s long-welded track began to come in, new and elaborate

This light riding van, DS53, was new in 1957 to run with a Wickham trolley.
Lens of Sutton

A Central Section relaying job about 1924, with the 'C2X' 0–6–0 in LBSC livery and the two riding vans lettered SR. Ready-chaired sleepers are carried on flat-wagons with removable side stanchions. *Lens of Sutton*

forms of PW equipment were developed. For the Bournemouth relaying in advance of electrification, in 1966, rail-welding equipment had to be borrowed from London Transport. For this work an unusual and no doubt temporary test-train was formed: a motor coach from Brighton Line 6-PAN set 3031 and a converted 'pill-box' goods brake, hauled by an electric loco.

In 1986 BR purchased 30 'Bruff' road-rail maintenance trucks; fairly normal-looking riding vans which had a built-in turntable, enabling them to stop on a level crossing and swing round, also bringing the rail guidance wheels into action. They were numbered 501–30, and Ashford, Eastleigh and Brighton got 526–8 in that order.

CRANES

There was a clear distinction between cranes which were more or less static (though wheeled) and those intended to run over the lines. In the former category come dockside cranes, cranes for moving fuel, ashes etc. at locomotive depots, and of course cranes inside locomotive and carriage works. In general, none of these received service numbers. The second category cover two sorts, the large breakdown cranes (mostly steam or later diesel) and smaller ones worked by hand which travelled to outlying stations to handle unusual loads or to deal with minor constructional work. These did carry service numbers, the match truck provided carrying the same number, but followed by SM rather than S.

The LSWR had numbered their seven breakdown cranes and 12 lighter 'travelling cranes' (hand-operated) in a separate series. The heavy cranes and their locations at Grouping were:

1	(SR 30S)	8w.	Stothert & Pitt	1908	Eastleigh
2	(SR 31S)	?	?	1880	Guildford
3	(SR 32S)	6w.	Dunlop & Bell	1885	Bournemouth
4	(SR 33S)	6w.	Appleby	1895	Strawberry Hill
5	(SR 34S)		Stothert & Pitt	1909	Exmouth Junction
6	(SR 35S)	10w.	Ransomes & Rapier	1918	Nine Elms
7	(SR 37S)	10w.	Cowans & Sheldon	1922	Salisbury

There were match wagons numbered 36/38SM, because cranes 6 and 7 had two match trucks; the jib rested on the first and the other formed a spacing wagon between the other match and the crane itself. Later most heavy cranes had bogie match trucks made from scrapped carriages.

These cranes were not of course used only on breakdown work; they came in handy for bridge construction and suchlike. Some jobs were one-offs; for instance the Bournemouth loco crane was at Wool on one occasion in the 1930s loading a number of World War I tanks without engines in them to go for scrap. In 1940 the Nine Elms crane had a trip to Leatherhead to load six 14-ton diesel engines off the wagons for the local waterworks.

Heavy cranes were offered by a small number of makers, either eight-wheeled with a bogie, or six-wheeled rigid, or in one case a four-wheeled rigid section with Bissel trucks at each end. They mostly had cylinders 8 × 14 in., one each side of the swivelling body, driving a crank-shaft off which

The Cowans & Sheldon 1903 six-wheeled crane No. 207S laying rails for the Tonbridge north curve deviation in 1934.   *L.T. Catchpole*

The Exmouth Junction steam crane 34S (LSWR 5), built by Stothert & Pitt 1909, working on the track after a mishap at Brentor, in 1927.   *Lens of Sutton*

Cowans & Sheldon steam crane 202S (former SECR L3) built 1899, clearing up after the accident at Swanley Junction on 28th June, 1937; 'L' class 4–4–0 No. 1768 is under the sheeting.   *Oakwood Press Collection*

Another view of steam crane DS202 after moving from Battersea shed to Gillingham; photographed on 23rd May, 1957. *R.C. Riley*

Taylor & Hubbard six-wheeled crane 1579S (1946) with a bogie match truck made from a carriage frame. *Lens of Sutton*

Track drainage work near Hildenborough on 13th February, 1938; there is complete 'occupation' as the crane is working on the other line. The mixed train of ballast wagons and LMS common user 10-ton wagons has a 'dance hall' van as riding van and a 'pill-box' goods brake attached to 'C' class 0–6–0 No. 1593.   *Author*

Former LBSC steam crane No. 17, built by Cowans & Sheldon 1898, as Stewarts Lane resident crane DS316, withdrawn in 1953.   *Lens of Sutton*

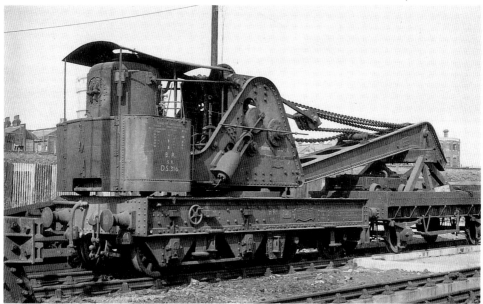

The Bricklayers Arms breakdown train attending a minor derailment near Southwark Park about 1946; the riding and tool vans are 1434/5S, of 1907 LBSC stock. The crane has left its match truck and been shunted over to the adjoining line to get a straight lift of the emu coach which had left the rails. *Lens of Sutton*

Former LSW crane No. 3, 32S, built by Dunlop & Bell 1885, erecting a footbridge at Pokesdown in 1931; with it are its match truck 32SM and 'M7' class 0−4−4T No. E36. *Lens of Sutton*

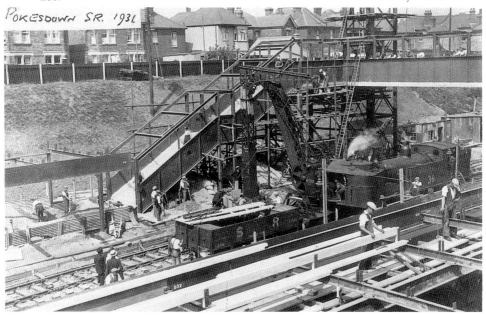

Lengthmen riding to work on a Wickham trolley near Teston Halt in 1934.   *Author*

The Bricklayers Arms heavy crane DS1197 prepares for a difficult lift after a derailment at Hither Green sidings on 21st February, 1940.   *R.C. Riley*

LBSCR Travelling Crane No. 19; somewhat heavier than some, its jib was rated at 10 tons. *Lens of Sutton*

Number DS429 was a hand-crane purchased by the IWCR from the Midland Railway; here seen at Newport about 1950 incorrectly painted as D429. *Lens of Sutton*

various power uses were taken by bevel gearing. Speed under their own power was about 2 mph. Similar machines were found on each railway, for example LBSC No. 17 and SECR No. L3 were both identical Cowans & Sheldon cranes.

The hand-operated cranes were sent to do awkward unloading at sidings not equipped with the static crane so many stations had. They travelled in the pick-up goods trains, and comprised the six-wheeled crane weighing about 16 tons, with a four-wheeled match-truck fitted with a crutch for the jib and a tool-box, which varied very much in design, from a little Mansell-wheeled conversion with ex-SECR crane 207S to converted 10-ton open wagons. Mostly the jib was rated at 10 tons. Clearly working these was a nuisance, for when in 1948 the static crane at Godstone was down-rated and unable to lift a tree-trunk, the Railway preferred to lose the traffic rather than send a crane.

Steam cranes, being on the whole rather more capable than i.c. engined ones, and also long-lasting because of small usage, outlasted in some cases the steam locomotives; the lure of steam therefore made them an attraction to enthusiasts, and one had a remarkable career. This was No. 199S, built by Grafton in 1917 for the War Department, sold to the SECR, passed from them to the SR and BR, and sold as DS199 to the Kent & East Sussex Railway, finally going to the Shackerstone Society at Nuneaton, having steamed under a total of seven different owners. When in the 1970s it became customary for the Region to have open days to display its equipment, performances by the remaining steam cranes were very popular. Three SR cranes, Nos. 81S, DS451 and DS1770 are now on the KESR.

Amongst hand-cranes, the most notable perhaps was No. 425S in the IOW, which was built by Kirkstall Forge in 1865 and was still at work at Ryde St Johns Road 101 years later.

Interesting too were the pair of breakdown cranes (hand-operated) bought for the Lynton & Barnstaple narrow-gauge branch from Cohen's War Surplus in 1926. They ran on two bogies, and the jibs rested on a common bogie match truck; the cranes were given the numbers 441/2S, and the match-truck 441SM. Although meant to form a set with a combined lift of 9 tons, most of the time they were separated and used as static cranes for goods loading.

The heavy steam cranes did not often travel far, as their home bases were well spread, but on one occasion in 1968 the Stewarts Lane crane had to be run to Eastbourne, as the Brighton crane was unserviceable. The following year the Eastleigh crane, running to Wandsworth to help with bridge repairs, was derailed at Hampton Court Junction; a heavy crane across four running lines must be a superintendent's ultimate nightmare.

Chapter Eight
The Southern Region Years

In 1948 it was decreed that Southern Region stock numbers should carry an S prefix, and therefore service vehicles were to have a DS prefix. This did not take immediate effect; at the time new service vehicles were receiving re-used old numbers, mostly low ones, and this went on until 1957; although a 3XXX series was started in 1950, re-use of old numbers also continued. When in 1952–4 a number of ex-SECR bogie brakes from the 1909 trio-sets were being converted to service vehicles, six for example took numbers DS3204–9, but others took numbers DS21/22/25/26 as late as 1954.

There was still a certain amount of oldish stock available; a ex-LCDR 6-wheeled van converted to 4-wheeled in the IOW, No. 1008, became DS3185 in 1950; DS3186 was a former LSWR 52 ft corridor compo. However the large pool of Maunsell passenger vans was raided from 1950; DS2–13 in 1953, DS138–156 in 1954–6 and DS157–71 in 1957, and many others, amounting by 1964 to 120.

The highest number in the new series noted was DS3323, a Wickham trolley. From 1958 yet another series, DS7XXXX, began. The 49 'Ironclads' which joined the service stock between 1958 and 1962 were partly in the old series and partly the new. After eight of the SECR's 1922 10-compartment thirds had been converted in 1959 to DS70052–4 and DS70064–7/9, there was little pre-grouping stock left, and 11 of the 1924 Maunsell corridor carriages were used in 1960/1, and 57 of the later ones in 1961–4, also seven of the bogie luggage vans.

In the 1950s a new 08XXX series was begun for 'internal coaches'. In 1962 two three-coach sets for 'Emergency Control Trains' were made up from Maunsell stock, numbered DS70159–61 and DS70162–4; they were for Government use to tap into the telephone system in the event of a nuclear attack and were supposedly 'hidden', the first at Tunbridge Wells and the second at Wimbledon and later Faversham. When the Ministry released them in 1981 it stated that they could be taken over by preservation societies, but in fact all were re-used by BR.

An unusual train around in the 1960s on the South Eastern Division comprised a diesel locomotive, brake van, tool and mess vans and a bogie tunnel inspection vehicle; this had been built in 1951 on the frame of an ex-LSWR corridor third brake, shortened to 37 ft 7 in., numbered DS658. There was a kind of hut at one end, and at the other a swivelling gantry which could be moved across so that two tracks were covered at once, with six men riding on it.

A further new use was 'Dormitory Coach'. The SR took over some ex-LMS 12-wheelers, DM198928–32 for staff sleeping; they were stationed at Launceston, Bude, Lyme Regis, Seaton and Wadebridge. In 1964 eight Maunsell coaches were lettered as 'Dormitory Coach', Nos. DS70136/149–53/212/3. The chance for yet another new label was missed in April 1957 when Cannon Street signal box was burnt out; 'Cannon Street Temporary Signal Box' was in fact LMR goods guard's van M730181.

Former Maunsell 3rd brake as Mobile Office No. DS70163, part of one of two three-coach 'Mobile Communications Centres' made up in 1962 for the Government for emergency use. One was stationed at Tunbridge Wells West and the other at Wimbledon and later Faversham. They were returned to BR in 1981. *Lens of Sutton*

A much-altered 'Ironclad' 3rd brake No. 3203 which became DS70017, the M&T van for Hither Green breakdown train in 1959. *Lens of Sutton*

It was 1959 before this 1897-built ex-SER guard's van was withdrawn, as DS1512. It was one of several steel-plated, two as early as 1915, and in 1939 became an ARP cleansing van, later an M & T vehicle. *Lens of Sutton*

Vehicle No. DS3202 was built in 1952 on an ex-LBSC 'B4' class tender frame; it was lettered 'Test Unit for Diesel-electric Shunting Locomotives'. *Lens of Sutton*

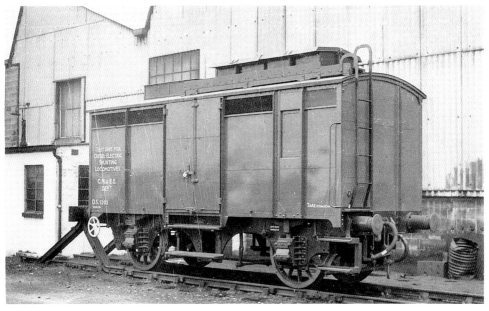

The mechanisation of track laying and maintenance had been proceeding, and a landmark in the early 1960s was the development by the Vienna firm Plasser & Theurer of a new self-moving tamping machine which could run to the site at 30 mph and lift and tamp sleepers at the rate of a quarter of a mile per hour, restoring cross-levels by infra red ray. These and similar later models ran in yellow livery. In August 1966 an Agreement was made with Rolls-Royce to supply Plasser & Theurer items; a new model ran at 40 mph. By 1975, with the introduction of the USP5000C ballast distributing and profiling machine, weighing 42 tons, speed 'on the road' was up to 50 mph. The DB number was quite small, usually shown on the cab side.

In 1965 the 0–6–0T No. DS234 at Meldon Quarries became the last steam engine at work west of Exeter; after the electric locomotive 74S at Durnsford Road was withdrawn in 1969 none of the old service engines were left. There was of course less need now, but after a while a service loco list of a sort was begun by BR, and a small diesel loco No. 97800 *Ivor* was stationed at Slade Green depot, and No. 97803 at Ryde St Johns Road; the latter had been No. D2554 on the Eastern Region and later No. 05 031. The much-truncated IOW line now had no inspection saloon; DS70008 which had been made from LBSC saloon S6986 in 1959 was withdrawn in 1967.

All the earliest SR departmental stock had been withdrawn before the preservation societies got into their stride, but in the 1960s much of what remained was given a new home. Ex-LBSC milk van DS1525 from Lancing was the subject of a public appeal and went to Sheffield Park, Bluebell Railway. In 1970 ex-LSWR milk van (4w.) DS1119 was purchased for the abortive Longmoor Railway Steam Centre, joining a similar van DS1686 which had been obtained earlier by a group at Fareham. No. 873S, a former 6-wheeled LCDR 3rd brake, was also moved to the Bluebell. A much later arrival there (1982) was ex-SECR brake 3rd 3410, which had been cut off on rail at Clapham Junction, renumbered from DS33 to 083180, and used as a classroom.

When in the 1970s some former Maunsell stock which had been converted to service use was becoming redundant, there was no lack of takers. The KESR took in 1971 DS70134 (2nd 1020), 081621 (1st 7400) and DS70201 (2nd 1346); and later DB975279 (saloon 7920). The Mid-Hants Railway took compo. brake No. 6601 which had gone to the Western Region as DW150386, and No. 6699 which had been No. 11 in the Chipman's weed-killing train, also DS70319 Bulleid coach No. 4211. The Swanage Railway acquired DS70175, an M&T van from Horsham in 1979, and 2nd brake 2768 as DS70172 in 1981.

The conversion of Bulleid stock had begun quite early, as stated in Chapter Two, with the 4-wheeled vans. Only five of the carriages became service vehicles on the Southern Region; they included DS70248, taken in 1966 as 'Teleprinter Office, Eastleigh'. No. 2526 after a period as a static vehicle was converted into instruction car ADB 975375 in 1974.

With the end of steam, there came also the end of converted tenders. Some of the last were eight 'Schools' class tenders which were converted at Ashford in 1964 into snow-ploughs. They were fitted with heavy dumb

Ballasting in the 1970s; a class 33 with six bogie bottom-discharging hoppers; no vans, for the gang have arrived by road personnel carrier; seen near Godstone in July 1974.   *Author*

A tunnel inspection vehicle No. DS658 on a shortened coach chassis, seen here at Stewarts Lane. The platform can be swivelled across an adjoining track to give complete coverage.   *Lens of Sutton*

Former Maunsell LVs were to be found in many parts of BR; here DB975568 is on a track-laying train at Westbury, WR in 1983.   *Author*

buffers at the 'engine' end, and a sloping cover built over the tender, with an adjustable ramp down almost to rail level at the 'business' end. They were numbered DS 70210/11/24–29; number 24 went to Eastleigh, 27 to Redhill and 25/9 to Salisbury; the rest stayed at Ashford. In 1967 Eastleigh Works also built some snow-ploughs, but these went to the Western and Midland Regions. A press release before the winter of 1968/9 stated that there were eight ploughs in the Southern Region and 71 country-wide.

An odd note was struck in 1965 when an enthusiast noted two ex-LMS tenders (Nos. 1484/1566) at Eastleigh, purpose unstated.

By the end of 1970, with the new series up to DS70319, numbering was switched to an all-line series begun by BR in 1967, Southern Region stock being included in a DB975XXX series. An additional prefix letter was used to indicate the Department involved: A for Mechanical & Electrical Engineers, C for BREL, K for Signals & Telecommunication, R for Research, and T for Operating Department. At the same time the 08 series was kept for 'internal' stock; this included an assortment of stock, mainly wagons, but also many carriages which were confined to use in depots.

In March 1971 two Service Vehicles went abroad; an Exhibition train was dispatched to tour Europe and included two Southern Region coaches and a cinema coach from the Western.

In 1972 'Open Days' at Brighton and Eastleigh included some Service Vehicles; in the former case they included the 80-years-old electric locomotive of the Waterloo & City line, No. 75S, and in the latter the Instruction Train 053, the LSWR carriage bodies of which were over 60 years old!

A sign that Service Stock had 'come out of the cold' for enthusiasts was the frequent references in the magazines to weed-killing trains. These were moving into the private sector; Chipman Chemical Co. of Horsham began by supplying tanks, then took over the trains themselves, running in 'house' livery of red and white, later apple green; a number of former SR vehicles were purchased, including two scenery vans. At first all the trains were worked push-pull; similar trains belonging to Fisons, which normally worked on the Midland and Western Region, were not. These were made up from former LMS stock and were occasionally used on the SR. By the 1980s the Chipman trains were being worked by a pair of class 20 diesel locos, one at each end, and these were put in store at Horsham with the trains after the spraying season ended. Chipmans had their own stock numbering system; some were replaced from time to time, and went on to a further life on a 'Preservation' railway. The usual make-up was a spraying or 'machinery' van, a carriage as mess van, four or five tanks and a luggage van for stores.

One former SR weed-killing carriage, DS70070 (former 6888) was noted on the Eastern Region in 1974.

When in 1990 the Inspection Saloon TDB975025 was repainted in NSE livery, it was shown off at a 'press conference' at Stewarts Lane; it was pointed out that it could be driven from either end, and was compatible with class 33/1 and 73/1 locomotives and most ex-SR emu stock.

One train always noted by enthusiasts was the Speno rail-grinding set. The USA/Swiss Speno Company had been hiring such trains to BR since

Service locomotive DS237 *Maunsell* at Chart Leacon depot in August 1964.
A.C. Ingram

Ruston & Hornsby diesel No. DS1173 at Hither Green mpd, September 1963.
A.C. Ingram

Fowler diesel engine No. 600S at Eastleigh Carriage Works, July 1959.　　*A.C. Ingram*

A new 75-ton Cowans & Sheldon diesel crane after delivery at Hither Green in April 1964, not yet numbered. Three match-trucks are provided.　　*A.C. Ingram*

1972; they usually comprised a locomotive, water/fuel carrier, and four rail-grinding cars each having six grinding wheels. They could travel at 30 mph, but at only 2 mph while grinding.

The change to long-welded rail had called for various new types of rail-carriers, such as DB975500–33, made up from the frames of 6PAN, 4COR, 4BUF and 4RES origin.

On 17th June, 1989 the 150th anniversary of Eastleigh Works was marked by the running of public trains into the Works, and the display included 0–6–0 works shunter No. 08 642 in special blue livery, lettered BRML Eastleigh Works.

A strange service requirement emerged in 1990, when a Drought Order made it impossible to operate the Ashford carriage washing plant, and also that at Ramsgate. Two surplus motor luggage vans towing two tank wagons each were dispatched daily to the railway-owned artesian well at Dover and thence to the washing plants.

The special efforts made on the Region to combat icing of the live rail and slipping due to fallen leaves has been covered in Chapter Six; that it was a serious problem was evidenced by Derby Laboratory sending a Sandite test train to the Sanderstead area on 9th November, 1987. Inter-Region running was exemplified by a train comprising two ex-Hastings demu motors, a trailer and a speed-recording coach, which was noted on the former Met &GC lines in 1986.

New types of vehicle included Mars Test Coach ADB970532, made from an LM 'Watford' electric coach, used on tests for Gatwick Railair services in 1984. A bogie test vehicle for the Channel Tunnel was made up from a class 33 locomotive and numbered 83 301, kept at Stewarts Lane. Rail cleaning car ADB977695 came from former class '202' coach 60525. From coaches of two EPB sets, 77102/3/6/11, a training demu was formed, numbered 939999, containing coaches ADB 97/688–91. Another example of the increasing inter-Regionalisation of service stock was the conversion in 1991 of former EPB set 5517 to a 'Brake Force Runner' for ferrying new class 456 units from York to Strawberry Hill.

The increasing sophistication of engineering work now called for mobile laboratory and testing gear which was too expensive to be provided on a Regional basis, and such stock was on a separate list of Research Department stock. This included only one item of former Southern Region origin: RDB975386 was a former Hastings line coach used as 'Lab Test 4' on a train testing 'tilting' mechanisms in 1974. Because it was so narrow, it could tilt without fouling line-side items.

Service stock today does not hide itself; all over the former Region the yellow apparatus can be seen, with just here and there a little in the old style, such as ballast brake noted at Three Bridges painted pale blue. Indeed the beautifully-turned out German 'Snow Train' was on display at the London Bridge Open Days in 1991.

By 1990 the last of the former Southern Railway service vehicles, mostly Maunsell vans, had almost all gone, many fortunately to private railways where they can still be found. As late as 1992, No. 374S, a 1919 SECR

Maunsell passenger van, was acquired by the KESR after 26 years of static life as No. 082757.

The days when 'conversion' meant just taking a vehicle out of capital stock and putting a stove in it had long gone, but 'second use' had not died out; the MLVs, now renumbered 931091–9/090, were dispersed as depot shunting pilots. In July 1993 former EPB set 6401 began a new life as Channel Tunnel Driver Learning Unit No. 931001, one coach, No. 77531 (now 977854) equipped as a mobile class-room. It ran in NSE livery; as of old, service vehicles use various liveries; the MLVs transferred to Strawberry Hill have one in so-called 'Jaffa-cake' colours and the other plain blue.

Changes have continued in permanent way maintenance; in 1993 there was a demonstration at Hoo Junction sidings of a train comprising 10 'Octopus' hopper wagons (Nos. DR92213–22), with generator van No. DC210306, which was authorised to travel as speeds up to 96 kph. In the same year, the Meldon Quarries, which had provided most of the ballast for the Southern, came up for sale.

There is still room for some individuality, as shown by the recent repainting of the Eastleigh Works '08' shunter in green livery with its old D3816 number, and named *G. H. Stratton* after a long-serving employee. It seems certain that the study of service vehicles will continue to be of great interest, and well recorded. When recently the Gillingham Sandite set No. 930007 paid a daytime visit to Victoria, it was duly pounced upon and photographed by one of today's Southern enthusiasts.

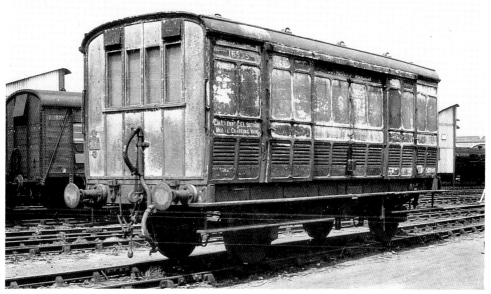

This Mobile Charging Van, No. 1653S, was one of a number of former LSWR milk vans converted; here it is in a mixture of peeled service paint and former SR passenger livery.   *Lens of Sutton*

Appendix One

Extracts from the Duplicate List

(Supplied by David Gould)

(A) THE LSWR SECTION

Nos. 01S to 023S were carriage lighting gas container wagons, all at that time single cylinders on frames from 4w. coaches and vans, except where noted.

SR No.	LSW	Built	Renumbered	SR No.	LSW	Built	Renumbered
01S	1S	1896		012S	13S	1898	2093S
02S	2S	1896	2092S	013S	14S	1885	2006S
03S	4S	1897	6w.	014S	15S	1898	2097S
04S	5S	1897		015S	16S	1898	2072S
05S	6S	1897	2095S	016S	17S	1883	2007S
06S	7S	1883	2071S 6w.	017S	18S	1885	2098S
07S	8S	1887		018S	19S	1883	2008S
08S	9S	1887		019S	20S	1881	2003S 6w.
09S	10S	1898	2001S 6w.	020S	118S	1890	2074S Double 6w.
010S	11S	1898	2002S 6w.	021S	119S	1886	2075S "
011S	12S	1898	2096S	022S	123S	1886	2076S "
				023S	124S	1889	2077S "

Note: renumbering took place in 1945. 015S, 016S, 018S changed to 6w. frame before renumbering. The numbers of the vans whose frames were used is known, but as cylinders were swapped around, cannot be allotted.

024S to 028S were vacuum cleaner vans, later transferred to V series:

SR No.	LSW	Built	Renumbered	SR No.	LSW	Built	Renumbered
024S	23S	1883	V4	027S	26S	1883	V8
025S	24S	1883	V3	028S	27S	1883	V9
026S	25S	1883	–				

There followed a batch of breakdown train vans made from 4w. and 6w. carriages:

035S LSW 50S 4w. guard's van, Barnstaple Jn
036S LSW 53S 6w. 3rd Brake 385, Bournemouth
037S LSW 55S 6w. GV 105, Bournemouth
038S LSW 56S 6w. guard's van, Strawberry Hill
039S LSW 57S 4w. covered van, Strawberry Hill
048S LSW 75S 6w. guard's van, Eastleigh
064S (LSW 140S) a 24 ft LV (5092) converted to a machinery van for Wimbledon ironworks in 1922
068S (LSW 54S) a similar van converted for electrical stores 1916
069S (LSW 60S) a 30 ft Brake No. 386 of 1884, Wimbledon Ironworks
071S (LSW 0578) a 3 cmpt 3rd Brake at Wimbledon, for Bridge Examination
073S (LSW 09) a 6w. saloon described in Chapter Five
077S (LSW 0110) a 4w. GV lettered 'Carriage of Stores between Eastleigh and Clapham Junction converted 1913
078S (LSW 29S) a 6w. LV of 1883, No. 35, converted 1915
082S (LSW 45S) a 4w. 22 ft LV No. 03 converted 1915
083S (LSW 5063) a 6w. LV of 1887 LSW 63, converted 1925
084S (LSW 5097) a 4w. LV converted 1922. Eastleigh and Durnsford Rd

The above were noted in 1929 in grey or black livery, except 071S, red; 073S still LSWR passenger livery, 035–75 brown.

Vehicle Nos. 085S–0105S were stores vans (LSW 90S–110S) made from goods brakes or covered wagons. The next two were interesting: 0106/7S open wagons with special buffing gear for attaching to Waterloo & City line stock in trains to Eastleigh for maintenance; they were withdrawn in 1935.

There followed some 300 yard and dock wagons, which were not placed by the LSW in their S list; some yard wagons at Eastleigh Carriage Works were lettered A to T, allotted 0218–0237S by SR, though they were withdrawn almost immediately. The SR inserted two carriage lighting gas container wagons into the series in 1925/6 Nos. 0499S and 0550S. The numerous old tenders used for various purposes, in an LSWR list and all from Beattie engines, with the centre axle removed, were also given a place in the 05XXS list. Some of these lasted a few years into SR days: 0521S at Barnstaple Junction, 0524S (LS23) at Wimbledon, 0529S (LS11), 0534S (LS18) and 0549S (LS19) at Eastleigh, and 0535S at Ashford.

(B) THE SECR SECTION

Some 40 four-wheeled M & T and Tool Vans, converted in SECR days from carriages of considerable age, appeared at the beginning of the portion of the duplicate list for the Eastern Section; these were all withdrawn between 1925 and 1938:

SECR	SR	Original	Form	Built	Service Use at Grouping
S1	0601S	LCDR		1879	Breakdown Van Tunbridge Wells
S2	0602S	LCDR		1880	Breakdown Van Stewarts Lane
S3	0603S	LCDR		1879	Breakdown Van Stewarts Lane
S4	0604S	?		?	Breakdown Van Faversham
S5	0605S	?		?	Breakdown Van Faversham
S6	0606S	LCDR		1881	Breakdown Van Gillingham
S7	0607S	LCDR		?	Breakdown Van Faversham
S8	0608S	LCDR	Pass. Bk.	1861	Breakdown Van Dover
S9	0609S	LCDR	Pass. Bk.	1861	Breakdown Van Dover
S10	0610S	LCDR	Pass. Bk.	1861	Breakdown Van Dover
S11	0611S	?		?	Loco. Dept. Ramsgate
S12	0612S	?		?	Breakdown Van Ramsgate
S13	0613S	?		?	Breakdown Van Gillingham
S14	0614S	LCDR	Pass. Bk.	1866	Breakdown Van Maidstone West
S15	0615S	SER		1864	S & T Tool Van
S16	0616S	SER		1864	S & T Dept. Tonbridge
S17	0617S	SER		1864	Engineers Dept.
S18	0618S	SER	4 Compt 3rd	1864	Engineers Dept.
S19	0619S	LCDR		1887	Engineers Crane Fitters Van
S20	0620S	LCDR		1879	Breakdown Van Tonbridge
S21	0621S	LCDR	4 Compt 1st	1885	Engineers Signals Dept
S22	0622S	LCDR		1885	Engineers Dept
S23	0623S	LCDR	3 Cpt 3rd Bk.	1890	Engineers Canterbury East
S24	0624S	LCDR	Pass. Bk.	?	Breakdown Van Gillingham
S25	0625S	SER		1865	Breakdown Van Hastings
S26	0626S	SER		1866	Breakdown Van Bricklayers Arms
S27	0627S	SER	2 cpt 3rd Bk.	1866	Travelling Paintshops Van

SECR	SR	Original	Form	Built	Service Use at Grouping
S28	0628S	SER		1857	Paintshops Van Ashford
S29	0629S	LCDR		1866	Breakdown Van Ashford
S30	0630S	SER		1857	Breakdown Van Dover
S31	0724S	SECR	Open wagon	?	Tunnel Examination
S32–5	0725–8S: timber wagons Angerstein's Wharf				
S40–1	0735–6S: sponge cloth vans from cov. gds.				
S52	0737S	SECR	Cov. Gds	?	Redhill–Reading, return Ashford
S53	0738S	SER	Bk. van 176	1863	
S54	0739S	SER	LV 186	1863	Gillingham–Maidstone West.
S55	0740S	SER	LV 27	1866	
S56	0741S	SER	LV 188	1863	Return to Longhedge Works
S57	0742S	LCDR	Cov. Gds	1882	Tonbridge & St Leonards
S60	0631S	SER		1866	Travelling Workshop,Angerstein's
S61	0632S	SER	Pass. Bk.	1856	Engineers Tool Van Strood
S62	0633S			1864	Engineers Dept Tonbridge
S63	0634S	LCDR		1881	Engineers Ashford
S64	0635S	SER	4 compt 3rd	1867	Engineers Painting Dept
S65	0636S	SER	4 compt 3rd	1865	Travelling Paintworks, Snodland
S66	0637S	LCDR		1877	Painters Tool Van, Longhedge
S69	0638S	?		?	Travelling Paintworks, Tonbridge
S71	0639S	?		?	Pneumatic Tool Van, Longhedge

All 4-wheeled passenger stock unless stated.

Early SER carriages which ended up on the SR Duplicate List were 19 ft 6 in. or 20 ft in length, (SER full brakes 18 ft), and 7 ft 3 in. or 8 ft 4 in. wide; built in or before 1866. The former LCDR carriages were more modern, 25 ft by 8 ft 6 in. (26 ft after 1880). Although both companies had some six-wheelers during this time, none were then converted. Outside builders used included General Rolling Stock, Oldbury, Gloucester, Shackleford & Ford, Brown Marshall, Metropolitan.

Vehicle numbers 0640S–0723S were wagons number W1–84; details of their origin are not known to the author. No. 0647S, which was a lamp wagon made into a yard wagon in 1929, was re-numbered from 175S (built LCDR 1888).

The remainder of the 700s were mainly yard wagons, but No. 0785S was a vacuum cleaner wagon (later V5), and 0756S an ex-LCDR horse-box of 1879 (No. 210) working for the Carriage Lighting Department.

From here on the list became more or less inter-Section; although No. 0816S was an ex-LCDR 4-wheeled 3rd, it was lettered for the Western Division and spent many years at Barnstaple Junction; No. 0813S, a former SECR tender, was noted in use at Brighton. Former SECR saloon No. 0824S was taken from capital stock in 1932 to work with Drummond steam inspection saloon 58S; it was a six-wheeled 1st class saloon and carried visitors around the new enlarged Southampton Docks, being withdrawn when this work was completed in 1935. Three workmen's bogie coaches, also for the Docks, appear here, Nos. 0853–5S, ex-LSWR 198, 247, 399 of 1894–6, converted in 1934 and withdrawn in 1938. From 0856S onwards to 0900S were all docks wagons used in the 1934/5 Southampton Docks construction.

(C) THE LBSCR SECTION

A large part of the beginning of the section was taken up by locomotive coal wagons with rounded ends, mainly used for ashes, former LBSC 01 to 050 (SR 0901–50S). However wagons 051–100 became SR 01002S–01051S.

The LBSC had a series for sludge and water tenders: No. 3 was an old Craven one which did not survive to SR days. Of those from Stroudley engines, 'singles' and D2 0–4–2s, the following were noted:

4	SR	0988S	London Bridge
8	"	0989S	Eastbourne
9	"	0990S	Eastbourne
10			Streatham (replaced 1926 by 0991S)
12			Brighton (replaced 1926 by 0992S)

These had all been withdrawn by 1931, though a few in the S series lasted a bit longer. They were followed in the number series by:

0993S,	a sand tender at Brighton, probably ex-Stroudley
0994S,	numbered 13 by the LBSC a former 3rd Bk., M & T
0995S,	a 3-compt 3rd Bk. (Stroudley) for M & T Outdoor Machinery
0996S,	a similar purpose, former coach
0997S,	from Pass. Bk. 100 (probably 2nd Bk. 1876) Loco. Running, Eastbourne
0998S,	former LBSC 09, no other details
0999S,	no details but located at West Croydon, possible Stroudley full bk.
01000S,	Breakdown van at New Cross Gate, from cov. wagon
01001S	Breakdown van at New Cross Gate, from cov. wagon

Numbers 01065S–01073S was a group of 6-wheeled double-cylinder gasholder wagons, the first five ex-Met. Dist. Rly, the last four being ex-Metropolitan Railway. From 1928 cylinders were swapped around, but the 1945 re-numbering seems to have been 2050/73/51/52/58/59/60/49/61S. All worked from Rotherhithe Road or Eardley in SR days.

Numbers 01113S to 01119S were LBSC stores vans, formerly 0101–4/6–8, all withdrawn before 1930. Former 0105 was apparently not taken on.

01113S	from	3rd bk. 150 in 1914
01114S	"	cov. carriage truck in 1915
01115S	"	cov. goods 3670 in 1915
01116S	"	carriage truck 10 in 1918
01117S	"	carriage truck 141 in 1918
01118S	"	mail van 401 in 1920
01119S	"	pass. bk. 327 in 1920

No. 01127S was a two-plank ballast wagon, apparently out of use before these were renumbered in the ED series. 01133–40 were Stroudley carriages on the Lancing Works train, renumbered 402–9S in 1929; 01162S was another coach on this train, but this time ex-LCDR, renumbered 417S.

The highest duplicate number noted was 01255S, an open wagon for an ARP train in 1944.

Tenders of 'Schools' class engines being converted to snow-ploughs at Ashford Works in 1964. *Lens of Sutton*

The commonest type of service vehicle in the 1970s was the Maunsell LV; here DS70223 from Mitcham stands in the Newhaven Harbour East Siding in October 1975. *Author*

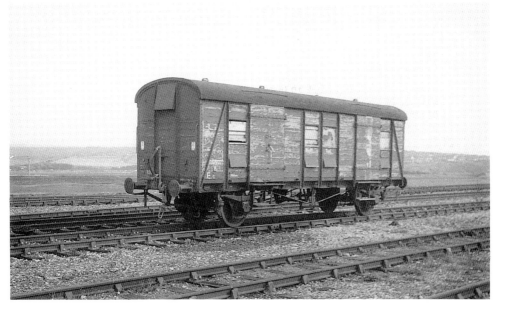

No. DS3212 was a riding van in the spare breakdown train at Norwood Junction shed. It was formerly SR 3336, originally an SECR compo with one 2nd and five third compartments.
R.C. Riley

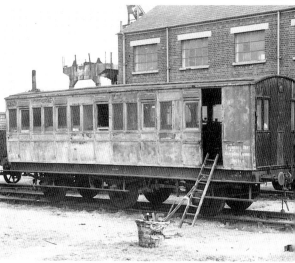

No. 873S was one which has survived. It was converted in 1935 from brake third No. 3630 (SECR 2781) and is here seen as an Outdoor Machinery van at Redbridge in May 1953. It was later-repainted dark green as DS873, and in February 1962 sold to the Bluebell Railway. *R.C. Riley*

Several of the 1900 'Metro' 3-compartment 3rd brakes were selected for Service use, becoming in the case of No. 3256 above, Mess and Sleeping van for the Signal & Telegraph Department, No. 1719S, in 1942; it lasted to about 1969. *Lens of Sutton*

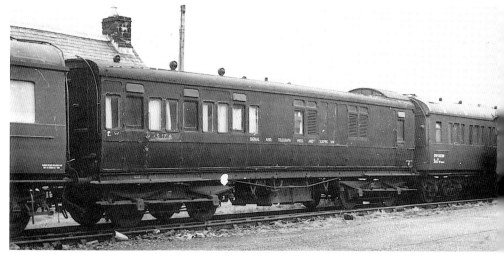

Appendix Two

Extracts from the Main Register (to 1946)
(Supplied by David Gould)

Insofar as this list had a pattern, it began with LSWR vehicles and continued through SECR and LBSC ones to a batch from the Isle of Wight beginning at 422S. However, by the time it was made up a number of ex-SECR vehicles were working on the Western Section, and many LSW items had drifted to other areas.

It began suitably with 1S, the bogie inspection saloon; other low-figure items included 20/21S, which were six-wheeled ex-LSWR milk vans, allotted to Eastleigh stores and 24S an ex-LSWR riveting van at Wimbledon Ironworks; cranes 30/37/44S have already been described in Chapter Seven. Nos. 62/3S, although on the Nine Elms and Eastleigh breakdown trains, were of SECR origin, the former ex-SER 33 ft 3rd No. 2065, the latter ex-LCD 28 ft Bk. No. 475. Nos. 66–73S and 88–90S were gas container wagons, and 80/1S were post-grouping steam cranes. No. 87S was a tender off an LSWR engine, 0473, but allocated to New Cross Gate Loco Running Dept.

Number 116S was a former SER covered van in the loco. depot at Ashford, later at Bournemouth Central; 121S–137S, gas container wagons, all 6-wheeled but some double and some single types. They were not uniform in appearance as they had been reframed between 1928 and 1942 on a great variety of frames from 28 ft to 33 ft.

There was a long series of ex-SECR vans made up from former passenger stock:

S No.	Former No.	Type		Location
141S	58	SER	4w. Bk.	Tonbridge
142S	119	SER	PO Van	?
143S	156	SER	4w. Bk.	Ramsgate
144S	159	SER	4w. Bk.	Slades Green
145S	164	SER	4w. Bk.	Maidstone West
146S	165	SER	4w. Bk.	Bricklayers Arms
147S	171	SER	4w. Bk.	Bricklayers Arms
148S	178	SER	4w. Bk.	Ashford
149S	306	SER	4w. Bk.	Hastings
150S	464	LCD	6w. Bk. Van	Dover
151S	465	LCD	6w. Bk. Van	Dover
152S	510	LCD	6w. Bk. Van	Reading
153S	511	LCD	6w. Bk. Van	Redhill
154S	516	LCD	6w. Bk. Van	Ramsgate
155S	517	LCD	6w. Bk. Van	Hither Green
156S	519	LCD	6w. Bk. Van	Ashford
157S	521	LCD	6w. Bk. Van	Maidstone East
158S	531	LCD	6w. Bk. Van	Tonbridge
166S	11	SECR	6w. Stores Van	Longhedge
167S	13	SER	4w. L. Van	Longhedge
168S	71	SER	4w. L. Van	Longhedge
169S	126	SER	4w. L. Van	Longhedge

S No.	Former No.	Type			Location
170S	192	SER	4w. L. Van		Longhedge
171S	193	SER	4w. L. Van		Longhedge
172S	339	SER	4w. L. Van		Longhedge
173S	0460	SER	4w. lamp carriage		?
174S	574	SER	4w. stores van		Ashford
175S	575	SER	4w. stores van		Ashford
176S	1933	SECR	4w. Pneu. Plant		Longhedge

All these were M&T vans, except No. 166S, which was a unique stores van built in 1905 as such, with semi-elliptical roof, one end door and centre double doors; and No. 167S, a 4-wheeled stores van converted in 1900 from a 4-wheeled LV. No. 173S was one half of a Williams 8-wheeled of 1851, later converted to an LV.

Nos. 180S–191S were ex-SECR shunting trucks, but these were scrapped early or moved back to capital stock and the numbers re-used; 188S was later a 4-wheeled LV (2022) allotted to 'Chief Engineer, Bellingham' in 1944. No. 195S was a saloon, a 6-wheeler built by the SER in 1886, slip-fitted; it was later SR 7765. Nos. 196S–199S were SECR coaling cranes.

In the early 200s series were a number of ex-SECR hand-cranes; No. 206S was unusual in having its small Mansell-wheeled match truck close-coupled to it. The contents here was very mixed; No. 225S was the ex-SECR Manning, Wardle already mentioned as posted to Meldon Quarries, while 226S was the brush-truck at Feltham hump yard. These came in the middle of a run of more Eastern Section M&T vans, as follows:

No.	Originally			Service Use
224S	LCDR	6w.	GV 483	Breakdown Van, Maidstone West
227S	LCDR	6w.	GV 479	Travelling painters' van
228S	SECR	6w.	GV 522	Telegraph Department Van
229S	SER	4w.	LV 270	Fitters' Lobby, Bricklayers Arms
241S	LCDR	6w.	GV 394	CEL Dept Stores Van
242S	LCDR	6w.	GV 484	Loco Running Dept West Croydon
243S	LCDR	6w.	GV 493	Loco Running Dept Fratton
244S	LCDR	6w.	GV 524	Loco Running Dept Fratton
245S	LCDR	6w.	GV 403	Breakdown Van, Salisbury
247S	SER	6w.	GV 506	Bridge Testing Van
248S	LCDR	6w.	GV 433	?
249S	LCDR	6w.	GV 545	Packing Van, Ashford Breakdown Train
250S	LCDR	6w.	GV 477	Tool Van, Gillingham
251S	LCDR	6w.	GV 481	Packing Van, Brighton Breakdown Train
254S	LCDR	6w.	GV 395	Outdoor C&W Dept Stores
255S	LCDR	6w.	GV 402	?
256S	LCDR	6w.	GV 400	S&T Dept Tool Van, Faversham
257S	LCDR	6w.	GV 538	Loco. Running Dept Dover
261S	LCDR	6w.	GV 392	Eng. Dept Electrification Stores
262S	LCDR	6w.	GV 405	Engineers Dept Stores

These conversions, all but one from vans of diagrams 878/9, were made in 1928/9.

Better known Nos. 243/4S were SECR bogie 3rd Bks 3319/3254 made into M&T vans in 1945, replacing the same numbers above; the 6-wheeled vans were withdrawn 1933–44.

Vehicles Nos. 292S–297S were a run of gas-container wagons, which had started life on the LSWR in the late 1880s (Nos. 2–7), but which had tanks and frames swapped around, now being double-cylinder 6-wheelers based at Rotherhithe Road or Eardley, 30–33 ft long; all were renumbered in the 20XX series in 1945.

The Central Section hand and steam cranes were mostly in the early 300s series, though 300S itself was a breakdown van converted from an LBSC 6-wheeled van, and running in 1931 in red livery.

Numbers 344/5S were interesting, having been the two LBSC Dick, Kerr petrol railcars tried on the south coast in 1905, and after some years of sporadic use, one officially an inspection car, were converted with roof platforms to service overhead electric wiring, based at Peckham Rye. No. 346S was a smaller Drewry/Baguley PW car purchased in 1915.

Several non-Central items were inserted: No. 349S was a tar oil-gas wagon lettered 'Return to Wimbledon Park Oil Works'. Mystery surrounded No. 350S which appears in the author's notes as having a clerestory roof in 1929, though the Register simply calls it 'Old No. 2' built in 1895 and located at Longhedge, withdrawn in 1930. Nos. 347–356S later became a run of de-icing carriages (see Chapter Six).

Numbers 365/6S were re-used in 1946 for two ex-SECR bogie brakes, Nos. 3350 and 3400. Following some 8-ton wagons (up to 367S), 368S was a hand crane. No. 392S was an ex-LBSC passenger guards van (SR 723), like 300S noted 1929 in red livery; 394S was another (ex-714), and then 395S–416S were the four-wheelers of the Lancing Works workmen's train already described. After 1934, Nos. 401S–413S were taken by the new bogie Lancing train.

No. 417S, an ex-LCD 4-wheeled carriaged on the Lancing train has already been mentioned. No. 422S was also a workmen's coach, but on the Isle of Wight, 'for the conveyance of the Company's servants between Newport and Medina Wharf'; it was formerly SR 4113, an LBSC 6-wheeled vehicle converted to 4-wheels, and whether its livery was changed is not known; it was withdrawn in 1932. No. 423S in 1932 was a tender taken from 4–4–0 B207, a fresh water tank for the workers constructing the Allhallows Branch.

This section of the register (from 422S to 445S) is especially interesting as it contained some items from the small companies:

425S, an 1865 hand-crane at Ryde (see Chapter Seven)

426S, another hand-crane, used at St. Helens Wharf, IOW

427S, an ex-LSW 4w. compo of the IWCR (No. 43) replaced in 1929 by ex-IWC guards van 17 (SR 990)

429S, the Newport travelling crane, ex-MR, ex-IWCR, was latterly painted as D429, probably because the IOW excused itself from painting the S in front of coach numbers after 1948, so DS429 looked wrong.

430–6S were former Island flat-wagons used in the workshops; all disposed of by 1925.

437S was the Freshwater Yarmouth & Newport's Drewry petrol railcar, used as a 'boat train' before 1923, now an inspection car, withdrawn in 1927.

438S was IWR guard's van No. 4 (SR 983), for Bridge Repairs.

439S, a long 4w. boiler-wagon.

440S, once a Somerset & Dorset Joint Railway saloon, was an inspection saloon, which after an accident was grounded at Broad Clyst depot.

441/2S, the narrow gauge breakdown-cranes (see that chapter) had a common match-truck, 441SM.

443S was a tank wagon on the weed-killing train in the IOW

444S, an M&T van and originally an 1864 North London Railway 4w. 5-compt 3rd, had been IWR 3rd No. 44.

445S was an M&T van from goods guard van 56036, allotted to Engineers but also used on the weed-killing train

Two numbers were re-used:

437S from 1939 was a Bridge Repair Van, from a 1920 LBSC cov. gds

438S from 1930 was a former IWR cov. gds. for the same purpose

Conversions of former passenger stock from 1930 to 1933 included:

S No.	Origin	SR No.	Purpose
458S	LCDR GV	419	Loco Running Dept, St Leonards
459S	LCDR GV	426	Loco Running Dept, St Leonards
460S	LCDR GV	447	Loco Running Dept, St Leonards
473S	SECR (4w) LV	875	Engineers Painting, Eastern Divn
474S	LCDR GV	430	C&W Dept Brighton
475S	LCDR GV	396	Engineers Dept, Central Divn
498S	LCDR GV	441	T&T Sidings, Woking
504S	LCDR GV	456	Stores van, Longhedge
505S	SECR GV	591	Bridge Repair, Eastleigh
508S	SECR GV	SEC 16	Loco Running Dept Wadebridge
509S	LCDR GV	408	Carriage Lighting Stores
512S	LBSCR 3rd Bk.	(185)	M&T van, Eastern Division
521S	LSWR GV	6	Stores van Wimbledon
524S	LCDR GV	424	Loco Running Dept, Dorchester
531S	LSWR GV	77	Stores, Lancing & Brighton
566S	LSWR Postal	4904	Emergency Plant, Eastleigh
569S	SER GV	632	Bridge Examination, SDJR
570S	LCDR GV	430	Carriage Lighting Stores
571S	LCDR GV	414	Loco Running Dept, Tonbridge
576S	SER LV 4w.	1938	S&T Dept Ashford
577S	LCDR GV	463	Loco. Running Dept, Horsham
584S	SER LV 4w.	1952	Stores, Epsom Downs
585S	SER LV	1953	Stores, Epsom Downs
586S	SER LV 4w.	1947	Stores, Epsom Downs
594S	LCDR GV	444	Loco Running Dept, Yeovil Town
597S	LCDR GV	449	Loco Running Dept, Tonbridge
598S	SER	1550	Cable laying, Brighton
605S	SECR GV	580	Stores van, Longhedge

All vehicles 6-wheeled unless otherwise stated.

There were some assorted items in 1930: Nos. 466S, and 467S were ex-Stroudley sludge tenders; 477S a steam crane on the Eastern (Grafton 1930) and 482/3S were Pooley Weigh vans, from covered vans 46117 and 45963, post-war.

Numbers 458–65S were re-used in 1947 for weed killing tanks mounted on 'A12' class tender frames, and 466–71S for Maunsell LVs in these trains. Tank wagons converted from engine tenders were:

S No.	Use	Tender	Purpose
497S	water	from B1 class	
501S	sludge	from B1 class	New Cross Gate
526S	water	tender 108 Bl cl.	Port Victoria
546S	sludge	tender 101 Bl cl.	Victoria
547S	water	tender 105 Bl cl.	Victoria
550S	water	tender No.1 A12 cl.	Eastleigh
564S	water	tender No.5 A12 cl.	Salisbury
565S	water	tender No.6 A12 cl.	Eastleigh
572S	weed killer	tender 126 (Adams)	Weedkilling train 1931
573S	weed killer	tender 138 (Adams)	Weedkilling train 1931
574S	water	tender No.4 A12 cl.	Loco Running Dept, Eastleigh
575S	water	tender No.10 A12 Cl.	Loco Running Dept, Eastleigh
588S	water	tender No.128 X2 cl.	?
602S	sludge	tender No.142 B2	Loco Running Dept, New Cross Gate

Vehicle 568S was a flat wagon in the IOW, and 587S a 6-wheeled gas container wagon working from Rotherhithe Road to Brighton and Lancing. In 1932–4 the vehicles converted were somewhat mixed:

S No.	Origin	SR No.	Built	Purpose
701S	LCDR GV	462	1897	Loco. Running Dept, Three Bridges
702S	LCDR GV	454	1888	Loco. Running Dept, Faversham
721S	SECR GV	605	1905	Traffic Dept stores, Mitcham
725S	LCDR 8w. 3rd	854	1897	Breakdown train, Bricklayers Arms
726S	LCDR 8w. 3rd	859	1898	Breakdown train, Bricklayers Arms
727S	LCDR 8w. 3rd	862	1898	Breakdown train, Bricklayers Arms
728S	LCDR 4w. LV	1786	1898	Engineers Dept, Central Division
731S	SECR 8w. L 3rd	878	1903	Breakdown train, New Cross Gate
758S	LCDR GV	423	1887	Outdoor Machinery Dept
762S	LCDR GV	427	1887	Engineers Dept, London East
769S	LSWR 4w. LV	1570	1912	Carriage Lighting Dept
771S	SECR 6w. GV	551	1903	Sevenoaks Cable T.
772S	SER 6w. 1st	7417	1895	Sevenoaks Cable T.
773S	SER 6w. 1st	7448	1887	Sevenoaks Cable T.
777S	SECR 6w. GV	576	1902	Eastbourne Cable T.
778S	SECR 6w. GV	553	1903	Eastbourne Cable T.
779S	SER 6w. 1st	7454	1888	Eastbourne Cable T.
780S	SER 6w. 1st	7413	1895	Eastbourne Cable T.
852S	LCDR 6w. GV	457	1888	Electric Lighting
869S	LCDR 6w. GV	411	1880	Loco. Running Eastbourne
870S	SECR 6w. GV	540	1899	Engineers Western Div.
873S	LCDR 6w. 3rd Bk.	3630	1894	Outdoor Machinery

No. 873S was sold to the Bluebell Railway, 1962.

In this part of the list were also steam locomotives No. 680S, and from 1947, Nos. 700S, 701S (see Chapter Five).

By 1935/6 use was being made of more modern stock for M&T vans:

S No.	Origin	SR No.	Built	Purpose
900S	SER Compo 8w	5255	1896	L.R. Stewarts Lane
901S	SER Compo 8w	5256	1896	L.R. Stewarts Lane
910S	LSWR 6w. LV	1634	1902	Eng. Ironworks Wimbledon
911S	LCDR 6w. GV	410	1880	Loco. Running Faversham
912S	SDJR 6w. GV	970	1889	Loco. Running Faversham
913S	LSWR 6w. GV	97	1896	Loco. Running Faversham
914S	SECR 6w. GV	569	1901	Loco. Running Eastleigh
915S	SER 4w. cov. gds	44792	1890	Sponge cloth van, Ashford
916S	SECR 6w.	4664	1905	Outdoor M. Three Bridges
917S	LSWR 4w. cor. gds	43528	1911	Pooley's weigh van
918S	LSWR 4w. PV	1383	1898	Eastleigh–Wimbledon–Clapham Jn
919S	LSWR 4w. Milk*	1251	1904	Lancing–Brighton stores
920S	LCDR 6w. GV	417	1880	Loco. Running Guildford
948S	LBSC 6w. LV	2159	1907	S&T Dept Guildford
949S	LSWR 6w. GV	81	1895	Breakdown Guildford
980S	SECR 6w. GV	593	1905	Carriage Lighting
981S	LSWR 6w. GV	89	1896	Loco. Run. Basingstoke
988S	LSWR 6w. GV	98	1896	Loco. Run. Barnstaple Junction
989S	LSWR 6w. GV	47	1894	Loco. Run. St. Leonards
992S	LBSC 6w. GV	858	1899	Lancing Works
995S	LSWR 8w. Cpo Bk.	6469	1905	Loco. Running Brighton
996S	LSWR 8w. Cpo Bk.	6470	1905	Loco. Running Brighton

*This was the LSWR's only 18 ft parcels/milk van.

There were some more locomotive tenders: No. 932S was off 'A12' class E603; 1038–41S were four weed-killing tenders mentioned in Chapter Four; 1054–7 were old tenders required to carry water from Ashford Works to the sponge cloth laundry at Ashford West. Two gas-holder wagons, Nos. 1048/9S, were inserted here. Number 1153S was a tender believed to be off 'K10' No. 135, for tar at Wimbledon Gasworks.

Some interesting carriages also appear: 1046S was former SER 6-wheeled saloon, SR 7898, and it lasted only four months as an ED S&T van. Nos. 1050–52S were three 4-wheelers of LCDR 6-wheeled origin, which had come back from the IOW in 1936 (SR 2477, 2489, 2495); though painted as M&T Vans, the compartment divisions remained, so it would appear they were really workmen's carriages, at Fratton. No. 1062S was ex-SECR bogie saloon, SR 7920, which had been part of the Royal Train; in 1948 it was in use as a mobile office at Wimbledon and it is not clear when it was transferred to service use. The number had been used before for an SECR 6w. GV (SR581), CME Stores, Rotherhithe Rd.

Carriage stock conversions in 1937/8 included:

S No.	Origin	SR No.	Purpose
1072S	SECR 6w. GV	481	Loco. Running Dept Dorchester
1085S	SR 4w. new	1937	M & T Van Crane Testing
1086S	SR 4w. new	1937	M & T Van Crane Testing
1087S	SR 4w. new	1937	M & T Van Crane Testing
1088S	SR 4w. new	1937	M & T Van Crane Testing
1110S	SECR 6w. GV	512	Weedkilling train
1151S	LSWR 8w. 3rd Bk.	2860	Loco. Running, Fratton
1152S	LSWR 8w. cpo Bk.	6542	Loco. Running, Fratton
1157S	SECR 6w. GV	560	Loco. Running, Norwood Jn
1160S	SECR 6w. Scen. V	4657	Carriage Lighting
1162S	LSWR 8w. 3rd Bk.	2888	Loco. Running, Ashford
1163S	LSWR 8w. cpo.	4968	Loco. Running, Ashford
1173S	SECR 6w. GV	620	Breakdown, Horsham
1208S	LSWR 8w. 3rd.	578	Engineering Dept
1234S	SECR 6w. GV	584	Weed-killing train
1235S	SECR 6w. GV	518	Welding plant, Eardley
1252S	SECR 6w. CCT	4675	Engineers S & T van Salisbury
1263S	LBSC 8w. 3rd Bk.	3897	Breakdown, Nine Elms
1264S	LBSC 8w. 3rd Bk.	3911	Breakdown, Nine Elms
1279S	LSWR 4w. GV	1000	For use in IOW
1280S	LSWR 4w. GV	1001	For use in IOW
1282S	SECR 6w. GV	627	Loco. Running Redhill
1287S	SECR 6w. GV	617	Bridge Repair Eastleigh
1298S	LSWR 8w. 3rd	244	Workmen's coach, Docks & Marine
1299S	LSWR 8w. 3rd	237	Workmen's coach, Docks & Marine
1300S	LSWR 8w. 3rd	404	Workmen's coach, Docks & Marine
1311S	SECR 6w. GV	628	S & T Dept Eastleigh
1343S	LSWR 8w. cpo.	4835	Breakdown and ARP
1344S	LSWR 8w. 3rd Bk.	2846	Breakdown and ARP
1345S	LSWR 6w. GV	86	Bridge Painters
1348S	LBSC 6w. GV	766	Lancing Works
1349S	LBSC 6w. GV	868	Lancing Works
1350S	LBSC 6w. GV	883	Lancing Works
1351S	LSWR 8w. 3rd Bk.	2819	Loco. Running, Salisbury
1352S	LSWR 8w. compo	4865	Loco. Running, Salisbury
1357S	SECR 6w. GV	477	Central Division

Numbers 1308S and 1309S were respectively a cinema van built in 1939 on an old underframe, and its generator van, formerly LV 1596 ex-LSWR. The pair was scrapped about 1973.

From the outbreak of War the conversion of carriages to service use was increased by the need for ARP facilities. Interesting conversions at this time include:

1427S, ex-SECR 6w. brake van 471 being given to the 'Road Motor Engineers Division'; returned to capital stock in 1942.

1434/5S, ex-LBSC bogie 3rd Bks 4002/3 making yet another change to the Bricklayers Arms breakdown train.

1438–40S, respectively ex-SEC vans 571, 478, 636, became ARP Emergency Vans at Ashford, Brighton and Bricklayers Arms, as Government property, being moved back to railway ownership in 1942.

1449S, the former postal van, has already been mentioned.

1450S, an SECR 6w. CCT 4670 was later a temporary office at Wimbledon.

1453S and 1454S were ex-LSWR 8w. compo (4917) and 3rd Bk. (2876) both for Loco Running Dept, Gillingham

1470S was ex-LBSC 3rd Bk. 3993 for Loco Running, Feltham

1471/2S were ex-LBSC 3rd Bks 3934 and 3901 at Feltham and Guildford

1476/9S were ex-LSWR Adams tenders converted for oil storage

In November 1939 a run of twenty-two 6-wheeled GVs were converted to Mess Kitchens or ARP Cleansing Vans; all were ex-SECR except 1513S (LBSC, SR 877), 1521S (LBSC, SR 905), and 1522S (LSWR, SR 73 which reverted to capital stock in 1940):

The ex-SECR ones were:

1506S	diag. 882	475	1514S	diag. 885	561	1527S	diag. 882	643
1507S	diag. 882	476	1515S	diag. 885	575	1528S	diag. 885	626
1508S	diag. 883	489	1516S	diag. 885	587	1529S	diag. 885	619
1509S	diag. 883	502	1517S	diag. 885	594	1530S	diag. 885	567
1511S	diag. 884	529	1518S	diag. 885	603	1535S	diag. 883	520
1511S	diag. 885	611	1514S	diag. 885	624	1536S	diag. 884	524
1512S	diag. 887	639	1520S	diag. 887	643			

1537S came from ex-SER mail van 4948, built 1896 (but given a later frame in 1942); to Mess kitchen 1943.

1542S could be said to be the first SR-built carriage to go into service use; however, though put together at Lancing in 1924 as compo 6233, it was on a World War I ambulance car frame.

1573S was intriguing, a former bogie LSWR brake van, SR 321 of 1906, it was labelled 'CME Service Vehicle No. 2; Shunt with Care. Not to be moved without authority.'

1579S, former LSW invalid Saloon (SR 7804) though in the Register as a yard wagon, was noted as 'For the use of the Local Defence Volunteers, Eastleigh'.

Vehicle DS1549 was converted in 1949 from a former LSWR corridor 3rd Bk. (3148) and DS1597 was an ex-LSWR corridor brake No. 3120 for the Ramsgate breakdown train c.1950.

Vehicles numbered 1601–14 were another run of ex-SECR GVs used as ARP Cleansing Vans:

1601S	former	616	Bricklayers Arms	1608S	former	612	Bournemouth
1602S	"	592	Nine Elms	1609S	"	582	New Cross Gate
1603S	"	558	Stewarts Lane	1610S	"	562	Sutton
1604S	"	604	Ramsgate	1611S	"	550	Salisbury
1605S	"	555	Ashford	1612S	"	583	Guildford
1606S	"	554	Eastleigh	1613S	"	597	Redhill
1607S	"	589	Three Bridges	1614S	"	600	Exmouth Junction

All these vans were of diagram 885; No. 1601S was sold in 1947 to the Derwent Valley Railway and later went to the Bluebell.

Number 1617S was a bogie LSWR GV 320 for the CME Western Division and 1619S was an ex-SEC 6w. GV 485, for Loco. Running Dept, Feltham. Number 1630S was a much-travelled carriage, an ex-LSWR arc-roofed bogie compo. of 1881, sold to the PD&SWJR (their 17), returned to SR, sent to IOW as 3rd Bk. 4106, returned to the mainland and allocated in 1941 to S&T Dept Blackfriars. Other conversions were:

1637S was a further cleansing van as above, ex-GV 638
1651S ex-LBSC 3rd Bk. 3948, to Loco. Running Dept Reading
1652S ex-LBSC 3rd Bk. 3987, to Loco. Running Dept Staines
1653S ex-LSWR milk van, 4w. No. 1434 to Mobile Charging Van
1689S ex-SECR 1st 7303, for Div. Eng. between Victoria and Banstead only
1690S ex-SECR 1st 7317, for Div. Eng. between Victoria and Banstead only
1695S ex-SECR 1st 7256, for Div. Eng. between Victoria and Banstead only
1696S ex-SECR 1st 7258, for Div. Eng. between Victoria and Banstead only

Eight more ex-SECR bogie firsts and compos and one 3rd were taken for stores vans at Eastleigh: 1697S (7287), 1698S (7296), 1699S (7334), 1700S (7363), 1705S (5393), 1707S (850), 1798S (7282).

Two bogie match-trucks for WD cranes came in here, 1722SM, 1723SM, when returned to SR becoming DS3180/1. Some more stores vans followed, made from ex-SECR 3rd and 3rd Brakes: 1730S (3331) (Fratton), 1731S (3348) (Guildford), 1732S (929), 1733S (948), 1734S (925), 1735S (927); all for Eastleigh.

Number 1704S should perhaps be mentioned, as this ex-LBSC covered van (46773) later spent some years beside the Crabtree Trust siding at Belvedere and was rescued in 1978 by the KESR.

Two six-wheeled ex-LBSC horse-boxes, Nos. 3316 and 3317, became Telephone Exchange Vans 1759/62S as noted earlier. DS1762−4 were later ex-Stirling water tenders at Exmouth. No. 1748S was a Booth's hand-crane, sold to the KESR in 1972, 6-wheeled 12-ton, built 1943.

Further thirds and third brakes were used:

1760S ex-SECR, SR 3272, breakdown van Reading, 1942
1772S ex-SECR, SR 864, stores van, Eastleigh, 1942
1773S ex-LSWR, SR 2944, breakdown van Faversham, 1943
1774S ex-LSWR, SR 2945, breakdown van, Dover, 1943
DS1776 ex-LSWR corridor brake, SR 3149, 1950.

Numbers 1791−4S were new carriage frames, which in 1943 were put to ferrying semi-finished products from Eastleigh to Brighton, and had their bodies fitted later.

In 1943 some ARP Clean Dressing Vans were made up, by pairing various saloons with SECR 6-wheeled GVs, which had vestibule connections added:

1823S	LSWR RC	7841	1837S	LSWR Sal.	7822	1844S	SECR 3rd	863
1831S	LSWR RC	7842	1838S	SECR 3rd	867	1846S	LSWR RC	7830
1832S	SECR 3rd	896	1840S	LSWR RC	7843	1847S	SECR 3rd	860
1834S	LSWR Sal.	7821	1841S	SECR 3rd	870	1849S	LSWR RC	7837
1835S	SECR 3rd	883	1843S	LSWR Sal.	7829	1850S	SECR 1st	7337

Apart from the first one, this represented seven pairs of dressing vans (the ex-RCs and saloons) and riding vans (the normal carriages) though riding van 1850S was in fact also a converted saloon.

Vehicles No. 1930–32S were three ARP Repair Train coaches, from SECR 3rds, SR 928, 932, 933. No. 1972S covered the underframe only of old 150S, which had been an ex-LCD 6-wheeled brake of 1879; this went to Lancing but was scrapped 18 months later.

Some War Emergency conversions took old S numbers; Restaurant Cars Nos. 7850/1/2/4 became 624–627S, and 7855–7 1628–630S, being used for mobile repair parties in 1944; these were 'Ironclad' stock built 1923–5.

A group of eight postal vans were given over to storing ARP equipment from November 1943 until 1946.

1882S ex-4922 at Windsor	1886S ex-4954 at Ford
1883S ex-4952 at Basingstoke	1887S ex-4906 at Botley
1884S ex-4957 at Lewes	1888S ex-4920 at Strood
1885S ex-4956 at Three Bridges	1889S ex-4951 at Stewarts Lane

As the War went on, more M & T vans were required to replace old ones or to cover new requirements; converted between October 1943 and May 1944:

S No.	Old No.	Type	Purpose or location
1872S	3274	SECR 3rd Bk.	
1873S	3283	SECR 3rd Bk.	Hither Green breakdown train 1943–60
1905S	2959	LSWR 3rd Bk.	Redhill Breakdown Train
1906S	2958	LSWR 3rd Bk.	Redhill Breakdown Train
1930S	928	SECR 3rd	ARP Repair Train
1931S	932	SECR 3rd	ARP Repair Train
1932S	933	SECR 3rd	ARP Repair Train
1954S	875	SECR 3rd	ARP Clothing Store
1955S	5280	SECR Compo.	ARP Clothing Store
1956S	5297	SECR Compo.	ARP Clothing Store
1957S	6155	LBSC Compo.	
1958S	7365	SECR 1st	
1960S	6609	SECR Compo Bk.	Mobile Living, Redbridge
1961S	3301	SECR 3rd Bk.	Mobile Living, Purley
1962S	3287	SECR 3rd Bk.	Mobile Living quarters, Woking
1966S	3244	SECR 3rd L.Bk.	Motive Power Breakdown Van
1967S	3257	SECR 3rd Bk.	Loco. Running Dept Plymouth
1970S	3294	SECR 3rd L.Bk.	Loco. Running Dept

In 1945 all remaining gas-container wagons were renumbered between 2001S and 2100S and 2101–33S added a few years later, all on bogie frames.

Thereafter until BR took over, and for a few years after that, old numbers were re-used. Some second uses are included in the above lists, but more were to come. These were not straight replacements; for instance an ex-SECR 'birdcage' third brake as No. DS132, Civil Defence Training School, took the number of a gas container wagon. In addition, over a thousand new DS numbers were created before the DS7XXX series began and many of these are quoted in the main chapter.

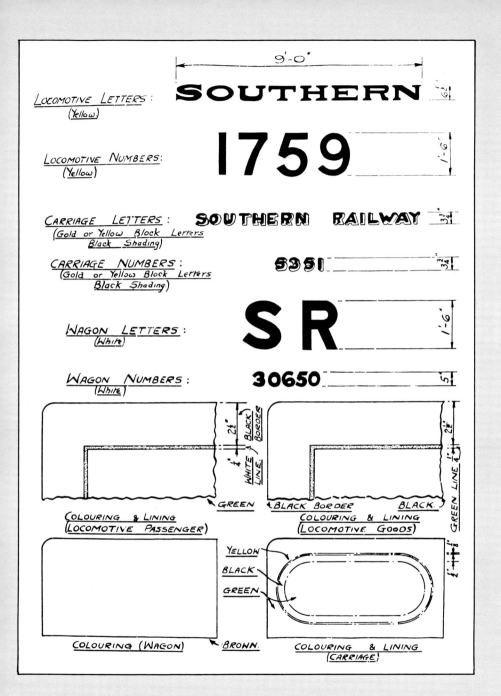

Sources of illustrations for tip-in drawing opposite

Drawings – a to f   After drawings prepared for the HMRS by H.V. Tumilty and based on photographs of 1918.

Drawing – g   Newton, J. Drawing no. SWC/D/3, revised issue 2 1970, previously printed with notes by A. Blackburn in Model Railway Constructor, volume 32, page 14, Jan. 1965.

Drawing – h   Tavender, L. Measured details taken 1951.

Drawing – j   Tavender, L. Noted 1950.

Drawings – k to m   Newton, J. Drawing no. SWC/D/1, revised issue 2 1970, previously printed with notes by A. Blackburn in Model Railway Constructor, volume 31, page 270, Oct. 1964.

Drawings – n and p   Based on photographs.

Drawing – q   Tavender, L. Measured details from grounded body at Wickham, 1969.

Specially drawn by L. Tavender, HMRS, showing the varied liveries. For use by railway modellers.